Alternative
Dispute
Resolution
FOR ORGANIZATIONS

Alternative Dispute

Resolution

FOR ORGANIZATIONS

how to design a system for
EFFECTIVE CONFLICT
RESOLUTION

ALLAN J. STITT

JOHN WILEY & SONS CANADA, LTD

Toronto • New York • Chichester • Weinheim • Brisbane • Singa-

John Wiley & Sons Canada Limited
22 Worcester Road
Etobicoke, Ontario
M9W1L1

Canadian Cataloguing in Publication Data

Stitt, Allan J.
Alternative dispute resolution for organizations: how to design a system for effective conflict resolution

Includes bibliographical references and index.
ISBN 0471-64295-9 (bound) ISBN 0-471-64323-8 (pbk.)

1. Conflict management. 2. Dispute resolution (Law). I. Title.

HD42.S74 1998   658.4'053   C98-931713-7

Production Credits
Cover & text design: Interrobang Graphic Design Inc.
Printer: Trigraphik LBF

Printed in Canada
6 7 8 9 10 SCI 19 18 17

For my wife Sari,
my children Jason, Melanie, and Lindsay
and my parents Bert and Barbara

Contents

Preface

Five years ago, the term "systems design" had little meaning in Canada beyond the fields of computers and engineering. Now, many Canadian companies are looking at how they can design systems to use Alternative Dispute Resolution (ADR) techniques to help them resolve both internal and external conflicts. I wanted to write this book to assist organizations to find appropriate and effective dispute resolution processes.

The pioneers in the ADR Systems design field are William Ury, Jeanne Brett, and Stephen Goldberg, whose seminal work, *Getting Disputes Resolved* (1988), first presented ADR systems design. Since then, a number of others in the

Many of the ideas in this book came from participants in our University of Windsor Law School/Stitt Feld Handy Houston ADR Workshops held for professionals, human resources personnel, public- and private-sector employees, and people from health, education, and labour sectors across Canada and in the Caribbean. I sincerely appreciate their contributions. I want to thank the University of Windsor Law School for entering into the joint venture with us to present the workshops.

General Richard Rohmer, Noel Rea, Frank Handy, Elinor Whitmore, and Lisa Eisen each reviewed a previous draft of this book and provided numerous insightful and helpful comments. I am grateful to all of them.

Karen Milner, my editor at John Wiley & Sons Canada, Ltd, gave numerous helpful suggestions and ideas that improved the book. I sincerely appreciate her effort.

I could not have presented any of this material to you without the groundbreaking work of Roger Fisher, Bruce Patton, Frank Sander, and other pioneers of ADR and negotiation at Harvard Law School. I learned many theories and lessons from these scholars.

I would also like to thank my assistant, Katherine Michanos, who provided hours of typing and editing assistance through many drafts of the manuscript.

I also acknowledge the cooperation of Keith Perrett at the Bank of Montreal, and Lori Rainone at the Ontario Human Rights Commission for providing permission to reproduce portions of the ADR systems that our firm helped them design, and Felicia Smith at the Law Society of Upper Canada for providing permission to reproduce a questionnaire for stakeholders.

Finally, and most importantly, I would like to thank my family—Sari, Jason, Melanie, and Lindsay—who provided a great deal of support, encouragement, and sacrifice. My parents, Bert and Barbara, and my grandparents, also provided tremendous support and taught me from an early age that there can be innovative ways to resolve disputes.

CHAPTER 1

Introduction to ADR

A company is having a dispute with its major supplier. The dispute has occurred as a result of the supplier's late delivery of an important order. The supplier claims that it is not responsible for the delay. Tempers flare and litigation ensues. Everyone hunkers down for a long, expensive fight. In the meantime, the company must look for a new supplier and cannot adequately service its own customers. There must be a better way.

⁙

*W*ithin the company, an employee is having a dispute with her manager. The manager wants the employee to work extra hours because of a downturn in the company's financial fortunes. The employee refuses due to child care obligations. Tempers flare and the *employee is officially reprimanded. The employee becomes angry and begins a work-to-rule campaign. There must be a better way.*

⁙

*T*he two senior partners of the company are having a dispute. One thinks that the company should make up lost profits by expanding internationally. The other believes the company should consolidate its operations and focus on the domestic market. Tempers flare and one partner stomps out of the office. The other partner withdraws and stops working effectively. No decisions are made. There must be a better way.*

There is.

Organizations can design conflict management systems to deal with both internal and external disputes in a productive way, and in a way that preserves rather than destroys relationships. Instead of resorting to litigation, strikes, work to rule, or withdrawing, disputants can use dispute resolution processes that will resolve their conflict efficiently and effectively. Designing an Alternative Dispute Resolution (ADR) system can help improve communication, reduce costs, maximize efficiency, and preserve or improve relationships.

All effective organizations have goals. Those goals may be to increase productivity, provide a pleasant work environment, improve teamwork and efficiency, empower employees, reduce costs, or increase profits. The organization accomplishes these goals through its corporate strategy or, for larger organizations, partly through its human resources strategy. ADR systems can help an organization achieve its goals. ADR processes have the flexibility to adapt to the organization and help it pursue its objectives.

Any organization can design a system, from two-person partnerships to large, unionized corporations. The formality of the system and its structure will depend on the organization's culture, budget, priorities, and goals.

Designing a system for effective management of disputes need not be a time-consuming, expensive, or difficult process, and it need not be overwhelming. For example, one person in the organization can be responsible for designing an ADR system, and can work part-time on the design. The new system can be implemented within a few months (or even weeks). New processes can be introduced quickly to alleviate immediate concerns as the organization moves incrementally toward an ideal system.

DEALING WITH CONFLICT

Conflict exists in all areas of life, and certainly within organizations. People disagree about many things: the direction an organization should be taking, urgent problems, long-term strategy, and even who should make the next pot of coffee.

The existence of conflict is not necessarily bad in and of itself. In fact, it is often a necessary catalyst that allows an organization to survive, evolve, and progress in changing times. Therefore, the goal in dealing with conflict is not to eliminate it but to respond to it constructively rather than destructively. Dealing with conflict constructively results in well-considered decisions that move the organization toward achieving its objectives. Dealing with conflict destructively, on the other hand, can result in bad decisions, low morale, and unhappy employees.

Successful organizations deal with conflict in a way that improves rather than destroys relationships, and that endeavours to leave everyone satisfied with the processes used to arrive at solutions, whether or not they agree with those solutions.

Why not ignore conflict?

When we avoid dealing with conflict (or ignore it), the root problem still exists. Conflict avoidance may provide a temporary recess from a stressful situation and allow people time to rethink their circumstances, but the underlying tension remains and may resurface. Even if it does not resurface, the disputants may be dissatisfied with the outcome and may harbour resentment that will manifest itself later.

Why not litigate?

Litigation (going to court) is the traditional approach to resolving disputes but it also has drawbacks, the most significant of which can be the cost of litigation, both in terms of dollars spent, and the time spent (or the opportunity cost). Because the organization must spend its staff resources to assist with preparing pleadings, gathering documents, meeting with lawyers, attending discovery, preparing for trial, and attending trial, employees cannot spend their time working to achieve the organization's goals. ADR processes can be less expensive and involve fewer staff resources.

Litigation also tends to increase tension between disputants, by engendering feelings of anger and hostility. ADR processes, however, need not be stressful and need not produce tension.

Litigation takes a long time. During this time there is uncertainty and the organization may be unable to engage in strategic planning. ADR processes can be quick and timely.

Litigation provides little if any opportunity for parties to vent frustrations; that is, to express their views to the other disputant. Although there is discovery, and direct and cross-examinations, there is never an opportunity to ask the questions that the parties (as opposed to the lawyers) want to ask each other and to say what the parties want to say. In ADR processes, however, disputants have an opportunity to vent and express feelings.

At trial, a judge must determine the winner and the loser, and there must necessarily be a loser in every piece of litigation. Judges must rule according to legal rights. In many ADR processes, on the other hand, the parties are not constrained by legal rules and can solve problems by developing innovative solutions.

In a trial, the court selects the judge. He or she may or may not understand the unique attributes of the dispute. Although judges act to the best of their abilities, they may lack the expertise in all areas to properly assess the merits of the claims being made to them, and therefore the results of litigation can be unpredictable. In ADR processes, those who assist with the resolution of the conflict can be chosen

based partly on their expertise and familiarity with both substantive issues in dispute and the ADR process being used.

When a judge renders a decision, the matter is not necessarily concluded. For example, appeals can prolong final
resolution of the dispute. And even when resolution is
final, there may be problems with implementing the decision. Although judicial enforcement mechanisms can be
used, people may attempt to avoid enforcement of a decision that they perceive to be unjust. For consensual ADR
processes, the disputants resolve disputes themselves and
identify their own solutions. They are therefore more
likely to accept the final decision and implement it.

In addition to the reasons for disputants to avoid the
courts, there are public policy reasons why reduced use
of the civil justice system can be beneficial for society. As
the justice system faces government funding cutbacks, the
courts have become less able to deal with the thousands
of cases that are filed every year. The increasing public
costs of litigation such as running courthouses and paying judges and court officials provide a reason for society
to consider alternatives to litigation.

SETTING UP A CONFLICT RESOLUTION SYSTEM

Neither ignoring conflict nor resorting to litigation will
always resolve conflict productively. That is why organizations should consider setting up a system to manage conflict
effectively.

Existing Systems

Some companies have an organizational structure to deal with conflict as it arises, whether there is a dispute among members of the organization or a dispute with another organization. They may have a legal department, a human resources department, or ombudspeople, for example. They may have a collective agreement with a detailed process. Other organizations deal with disputes as they arise, with little or no structure. Few organizations, however, have done an analysis of the kinds of disputes that arise to determine whether the processes and structures that they use are the most effective and efficient in achieving the organization's goals. Some organizations are unaware of their options for dispute resolution, never mind the costs and benefits of the various options. Where organizations have disputes with each other, they may automatically sue rather than explore cheaper and faster ADR processes that may preserve their relationship.

A unionized environment will likely have a system established through the collective agreement. However, that does not mean that a unionized workplace should not do a systems design analysis to consider how to improve the system. Union and management will need to work together to design processes that benefit the people both inside and outside the organization.

UNION CAN WORK WITH MANAGEMENT

The CBC television and radio station in Windsor, Ontario, is a unionized workplace facing significant conflict arising out of budget cuts. To deal with the conflict, management and union leaders decided to set up a new system. This system involved the establishment of a joint management/union decision-making team, and required that employees and managers participate in negotiation training. As a result, the CBC developed a system in which disputants attempted to negotiate a resolution to disputes and, if they could not, they submitted the issue to the joint union/management team which made a final decision. With this system, CBC Windsor reduced tension and avoided further volatile work disruptions.

What if you don't have a system?

Some organizations have a sophisticated system for resolving conflict. Many do not. Nevertheless, those organizations that do not have a formal system for dealing with conflict to resolve their dispute likely have an informal system in place, even if they don't realize it. It may be that a manager unilaterally resolves all conflict; or employees may be required to "work it out" themselves; or the company president may call the company lawyer immediately upon learning of a potential dispute. These are all examples of an organization's existing dispute resolution system.

Do small organizations need ADR systems?

Even two-person operations need an ADR system, though the system need not be sophisticated. How should disputes be resolved if the two individuals disagree? Should one person ultimately decide all issues? Should decisions require both people to agree? Should a third party decide? Although the answers to these questions will vary depending on the individuals and the organization involved, the questions are important nonetheless. The two individuals should consider these questions before conflict strains their relationship and poisons their work environment.

Regardless of the size of the organization or whether processes exist to resolve conflict, an organization can use a well-thought-out ADR system to achieve its goals.

ADR SYSTEMS DESIGN

ADR systems design is an attempt to match the appropriate dispute resolution process with the type of dispute, and with the culture of an organization. It is an analysis that attempts to produce a dispute resolution structure that is appropriate for the organization and cost effective. At the same time, systems design provides a structure through which binding decisions can be reached where necessary, if the disputants cannot agree on a resolution.

Because there is no cookie-cutter solution to all disputes, the organization must assess its needs to determine which processes are appropriate in particular circumstances and how they can best be incorporated into the organization's culture.

When is Systems Design Appropriate?

For an organization to find a better way to resolve its internal and external disputes, it must first recognize that it has disputes, and must then commit itself to achieving a more effective way to deal with its conflict. The decision-makers in the organization need to decide that the time is right to examine (or re-examine) the way that the organization resolves conflict.

Unfortunately, organizations that look for new ways to resolve their disputes are often organizations in a state of stress. The level of conflict is often at unacceptable levels, and sometimes conflict is not getting resolved at all, never mind effectively. Dispute resolution systems design becomes necessary to douse the flames of existing fires.

An organization need not, however, wait until it is in distress to look for an appropriate dispute resolution. The best time, in fact, for organizations to look at systems design is before a crisis has arisen, when conflict has not yet manifested itself. For example, an engaged couple enters into a prenuptial agreement not because they want to separate or anticipate divorce but rather because they want to prepare themselves, at a time when they are not fighting, to have an approach to resolving any issues that may arise if a separation or divorce occurs.

All organizations will benefit from considering whether there may be more appropriate ways to resolve disputes. Even if no process is found that can improve the existing structures, the exercise of considering appropriate processes will still help an organization assess its sources of its conflict, and may lead to a better understanding of the conflict.

GOALS FOR AN ADR SYSTEM

An organization that is considering the implementation of an ADR system will need to think about why it wants or needs the system. It will need to consider how it could be better off with an ADR system; that is, what criteria it will use to determine whether the systems design process has achieved its objectives. Although organizational goals vary, there are some common to most organizations.

Reduce Time and Cost

Often, the motivation for engaging in ADR systems design is to reduce the costs and time involved in resolving disputes. Organizations are constantly searching for ways to reduce costs, provided those reductions do not create more problems than they eliminate. If a new dispute resolution system can reduce costs and achieve outcomes that are just as good as those achieved under the previous system, that in and of itself may make the new system desirable.

A simple commercial lawsuit can cost more than $40,000. Complex litigation can cost hundreds of thousands of dollars. An ADR system can include processes that cost a small fraction of the litigation, and yet produce as good or even better results.

Similarly, organizations are constantly searching for ways for employees to use their time more productively. For every minute that an employee spends in an unproductive attempt to resolve conflict, that employee is not working to achieve the organization's goals (whether they be to make a profit, or some other objective).

An ideal ADR system reduces both the costs and time involved with dispute resolution processes and results in more satisfactory outcomes for disputants.

Improve or Maintain the Relationship

In situations where the members of an organization who are embroiled in a dispute have an ongoing relationship, the conflict resolution system should allow them to work through their difficulties in a productive way that does not destroy their relationship. It will not help an organization to provide a dispute resolution process that leaves people who work together angry and frustrated with either the result or the process itself. After acrimonious litigation or arbitration, for example, disputants rarely want to put the past behind them and work cooperatively.

In an ideal dispute resolution system, the disputants will have processes that will allow them to improve rather than simply maintain their relationship. If, in the context of resolving the dispute, the disputants learn information that will allow them to work more effectively in the future, they will be able to move forward after the dispute in a more productive way.

Satisfactory Outcome

The outcome of disputes must be satisfactory, both to the disputants and the organization. Regardless of the process used, the solution must solve the problem that exists. A dispute resolution system must move parties toward workable, durable, and implementable outcomes. The processes used must also yield substantive outcomes that support the organization's goals, whatever they may be.

An organization should not design a system that removes from disputants statutory rights to judicial relief. That is, if legislation grants disputants the right to have a particular grievance heard by a judge or other tribunal, the new system should not remove those rights. Instead, the system should work within existing legislative structures. For example, if an organization sets up a system to address human rights violations, it should operate within the confines of human rights legislation and obviously should comply with constitutional freedoms.

Deal with Emotions

The processes chosen should give the disputants an outlet to discuss their frustrations. The cathartic experience of venting emotions in a non-threatening environment is essential for the disputants to deal with the impact of the conflict on both them and their families, and in order for the disputants to be satisfied with the outcome. A disputant may be unable to deal with issues until he or she is satisfied that the other person has listened to his or her point of view. Litigation and arbitration, for example, do not provide an opportunity for venting and expressing emotions.

Avoid Future Disputes

A dispute resolution system must recognize that the process used for the resolution of a particular conflict can also have future implications. That is, if disputants learn techniques that can resolve disputes effectively and without damaging relationships, they can use these techniques when they become involved in future conflict. These processes can provide a framework to deal with other, unanticipated disputes.

Furthermore, where there are recurring disputes, the system may be able to take advantage of the fact that there have been resolutions in the past to provide guidance for the future. Precedents can assist disputants to learn from experience and create expectations in the dispute resolution process.

WHAT IS ADR?

Alternative Dispute Resolution (ADR) is a term that has received much attention in recent years. ADR is a spectrum of processes, other than litigation, that can be used to resolve disputes. Some proponents have suggested that ADR stands for Appropriate Dispute Resolution since the processes used should be appropriate to the conflict that has developed.

The ADR spectrum of processes includes negotiation, mediation, arbitration, and a number of other processes, some of which are variations or combinations of negotiation, mediation, and arbitration.

Processes in the spectrum vary in terms of the amount of time the process takes, the cost of participating in the process, the control of the disputants in determining the outcome of the process, the degree of involvement of neutral third parties in the process, and the likelihood that the disputants' relationships will be preserved at the end of the process.

The Types of ADR

The following ADR processes are presented in the order they appear in the spectrum, moving from processes that are shorter, less expensive, more in control of the disputants, and often better for the preservation of their relationship, to longer, more expensive, relationship-damaging processes where neutral third parties retain control. This list of processes is illustrative and not exhaustive. A number of the processes are discussed in more detail in later chapters.

Conflict Prevention — If a conflict can be prevented, there will be no need for a process to resolve the dispute. Organizations can, for example, provide employees with dispute prevention training to avoid or prevent conflict.

Partnering — One form of conflict prevention is partnering, a process often associated with the construction industry. Under this approach, before a project begins, the contractor, sub-contractors, architect, trades, and sub-trades all decide how disputes will be resolved if they arise during construction. Regardless of the methods they choose, they agree that construction of the project will not stop during dispute resolution.

Self-help — If disputants are not confident that an appropriate process exists to resolve their dispute, they may take matters into their own hands and attempt to resolve the situation themselves. Self-help could involve a physical confrontation, a strike, or sabotage.

Negotiation — Negotiation is communication between individuals for the purpose of arriving at a mutually agreeable solution that is better for both individuals than no resolution. In negotiation, the disputants themselves attempt to resolve the dispute. Negotiation is discussed further in Chapter 8.

Mediation — Where the disputants cannot negotiate a solution to the problem, they may engage the assistance of a neutral third party or mediator to assist them to overcome the barriers to a negotiated agreement. The parties remain ultimately responsible for deciding whether they wish to enter into an agreement to resolve their dispute. Mediation is discussed in Chapter 9.

Conciliation — One model of mediation requires that the disputants remain in separate rooms while the mediator shuffles back and forth between the rooms. This process is sometimes called conciliation or shuttle diplomacy. The mediator (or conciliator) may exchange offers between the disputants or may engage in private discussions with the disputants to learn facts that may assist him or her to settle the dispute.

Facilitation — A facilitator helps people in a meeting to communicate more effectively and to reach consensus. The facilitator ensures that one person speaks at a time, that everyone has an opportunity to be heard, and that the participants remain focused on issues to be resolved.

Med/Arb(Mediation/Arbitration) — Not all mediations result in agreement. As a result, a process called Med/Arb has developed where the disputants agree at the outset that if the mediation fails to result in agreement, the mediator or another neutral third party will act as an arbitrator and be empowered to reach a binding decision for the disputants. Med/Arb is discussed in Chapter 10.

Mini-trials — Where disputing companies have an ongoing relationship, they may decide to have a private mini-trial. In that process, disputants or their lawyers present brief arguments to senior representatives of the disputing companies who sit together with a respected neutral. The representatives and the neutral hear a summary of the case and then privately discuss possible settlement options. If they cannot agree, the neutral may provide an advisory opinion about the possible outcome in court. In a judicial mini-trial, a judge hears the case summaries from disputants and then works with them to resolve the dispute. Mini-trials are discussed in Chapter 10.

Early Neutral Evaluation — If disputants cannot agree on which disputant would be successful at arbitration or litigation, they may engage the services of a respected neutral third party who could provide an opinion on the likely outcome of their case, if it proceeded to arbitration or trial. A common example of early neutral evaluation is the pre-trial in the civil litigation context. Early neutral evaluation is discussed in Chapter 10.

Arbitration — In an arbitration, a neutral person (or panel) decides the outcome of the dispute. The decision is binding on the disputants. Arbitration is also discussed in Chapter 10.

Litigation — If the disputants cannot agree on another process, they can have access to courts, with the advantages and disadvantages inherent in.

INCORPORATING ADR INTO THE SYSTEM — THE "DIRECT" APPROACH

When disputes arise, they must be dealt with directly. Disputants may want to delay dealing with the conflict in the hope that the dispute will simply go away. However, avoiding conflict will not resolve the dispute and it will not help the organization to evolve. An effective ADR system should provide disputing parties with direct access to processes that can assist them to resolve their dispute effectively.

"DIRECT" is also an acronym for a framework for designing an effective ADR system. DIRECT stands for Diagnosis, Interests, Rights, Exits and re-entries, Creativity, and Training and evaluation.

Diagnosis

The first step in an ADR systems design is to diagnose the types of conflict and identify the approaches that the organization currently takes to deal with them. Effective dispute resolution processes should be maintained while ineffective processes should be replaced. Diagnosis is discussed in detail in Chapters 3 to 6.

Interests

Significant advantages are associated with people resolving their disputes by focusing on their wants, needs, desires, or interests rather than resorting to power or to their legal rights. Generally, disputes are resolved more effectively and satisfactorily for disputants if they use an interest-based approach to the resolution of conflict. Interest-based dispute resolution processes are discussed in Chapters 7 to 9.

Rights

If interest-based approaches to resolving conflict are unsuccessful or inappropriate, organizations can resolve disputes by having a determination of rights—a finding of who is right and who is wrong—using an objective person or standard. That does not necessarily mean that the disputants must end up in court. A number of other rights-based approaches to dispute resolution can be employed to resolve an outstanding dispute. Rights-based processes are discussed in Chapter 10.

Exits and re-entries

When one approach to resolving a conflict fails, there can be a number of reasons why. It could be that the approach or the timing is wrong. For example, the disputants (or one of them) may not be ready to resolve the dispute, either because not enough information is available to allow them to make necessary decisions comfortably, or because the emotions are too strong since the event causing the dispute occurred so recently.

It may be appropriate, therefore, to exit from a particular dispute resolution process, and try again, perhaps after a cool-down period. Exits and re-entries from dispute resolution processes are discussed in Chapter 11.

Creativity

Difficulties arise in the design of every ADR system. One of the most exciting aspects of dispute resolution systems design is the opportunity to be creative, even if the creativity runs contrary to traditional approaches to dispute resolution. There are no unbreakable rules in ADR systems design. Chapter 12 explores some creative options that can be used to overcome obstacles in ADR systems design.

Training and evaluation

The best system will never achieve its goals if the stakeholders do not understand it, if they feel excluded from the process of designing it, or if they cannot participate effectively in it. As a result, an organization with a new ADR system may need to allow some of its employees to participate in ADR training and education to familiarize themselves with the new processes and facilitate their use of these processes. ADR education and training are discussed in Chapter 13.

Chapter 13 also discusses the evaluation of an ADR system. An evaluation can clarify whether the ADR system is working effectively or whether further refinements are required. It may be appropriate to implement and evaluate a pilot project to test some of the new ideas and adjust the system before it is introduced throughout the organization.

SOME EXAMPLES OF ADR SYSTEMS DESIGN

Although I will present ideas from a number of ADR systems at various points in the book, for illustration purposes, I have selected two systems design projects that I have worked on to present in detail. They are presented at the end of each chapter. One of the systems that I explore in detail is designed for the Bank of Montreal and the other is designed for the Ontario Human Rights Commission. Excerpts of Procedures Manuals for the two systems are presented in Appendices B and C.

Case Study: The Bank of Montreal Project

In 1995, the Canadian Bankers Association decided that the Canadian chartered banks should offer mediation programs to deal with disputes between the banks and their small business customers arising from the reduction or withdrawal of credit. Each bank would be required to offer a form of mediation to its customers in the event of a dispute.

Each bank, including the Bank of Montreal, then had to decide how to incorporate mediation into its existing dispute resolution system.

Case Study:
Ontario Human Rights Commission

The Ontario Human Rights Commission (OHRC) investigates complaints of discrimination and human rights violations in Ontario. If the investigation identifies that the discrimination may have occurred, a hearing is held before OHRC Commissioners to determine whether there has been discrimination, and if so, the appropriate remedy to be imposed.

In 1997, the OHRC decided to investigate whether ADR processes could be used to better resolve the conflicts that it investigates and adjudicates.

S U M M A R Y
INTRODUCTION

- conflict allows organizations to evolve and progress if it is handled productively
- ignoring conflict allows the dispute to fester
- litigating can be expensive, time-consuming, unpredictable, and damaging to the relationship

ADR SYSTEMS DESIGN

- systems design is an attempt to design processes that are appropriate for the organization
- any organization can benefit from an appropriate dispute resolution system
- the system can utilize any existing processes that are effective
- the system should not remove statutory rights to judicial remedies
- systems design analysis can occur at any time, not only when the organization is in distress
- the new system should improve the existing system for resolving conflicts

GOALS FOR A DISPUTE RESOLUTION SYSTEM

An organization may want an ADR Stystem to:
- reduce time and costs for dispute resolution
- maintain or improve the disputants' relationship
- ensure that the outcome of the system is workable, durable, and implementable

- allow the expression of emotions
- develop a process that people can learn from

ADR

- ADR is a series of processes that are alternatives to litigation
- ADR processes include prevention, negotiation, mediation, facilitation, and arbitration

DESIGNING AN ADR SYSTEM

- use the DIRECT approach
  - **D**iagnosis
  - **I**nterest-based processes first
  - **R**ights-based processes later
  - have **E**xits and re-entries
  - use **C**reativity to solve problems
  - use of **T**raining and evaluation

CHAPTER 2

Diagnosis

THE SYSTEM DESIGN TEAM

As discussed in Chapter 1, designing an ADR system need not be an overwhelming task. For smaller organizations, one person can be charged with designing the ADR system. Larger organizations, however, should establish an ADR systems design team where budget and time permit. The team should be composed of individuals who have the time, expertise, and inclination to carry out the design of the system. The team could include members of the organization's legal department (if one exists), human resources personnel, senior executives, external ADR consultants, union representatives, and others involved in resolving organizational disputes. For the purposes of our discussion, I will refer to the systems design team even though the team may be composed of only one individual (for smaller organizations).

Where an organization has employees or managers who oppose the introduction of new processes for dispute resolution, the organization should encourage some of those individuals to join the team and participate in the design process.

Some people are naturally resistant to change. They are comfortable with the status quo and therefore may resist change simply because it does not reflect the way they have always done things. These people need to be consulted and their concerns addressed directly, so that they are reassured that they are not being ignored by those who design the dispute resolution system. The more they can be involved in the design process, and the more input they can have in the ultimate system, the more likely they will accept and agree to work within the new system.

Ideally, the team should also include an external ADR consultant. This individual can provide guidance with respect to appropriate uses of ADR processes, and can assess the design team's decisions objectively. Although the consultant should not make decisions, he or she should facilitate discussions and provide information, opinions, and guidance.

A retainer for a consultant to design a complete system for a large organization can range from $25,000 to $50,000. Smaller organizations may decide to retain a consultant on an hourly basis to review, critique, and assess a system. Hourly rates for consultants range from $150 to $300 per hour.

ANY RECOMMENDATIONS SHOULD IMPROVE THE EXISTING SYSTEM

A new dispute resolution system should be implemented only if it will produce tangible improvements to the existing system. If aspects of the existing dispute resolution system work effectively, those aspects should be incorporated into the new system.

Systems design is not taking specific ADR processes and applying them to a situation; rather, it is assessing the needs of the organization, determining what is working effectively, and changing what needs to be changed. Existing processes should not be discarded simply for the purpose of change. In fact, the systems design team will want to use everything that is effective in the existing dispute resolution structure, if possible.

The members of the design team will need to develop some expertise and understanding about the organization and its dispute resolution requirements. This can be done in two ways. The first approach is to review written material that may be of assistance. This could include literature about the current system (including any material in any collective agreements), written material about the disputes themselves and details of resolutions, and any studies or reports prepared about the organization and its disputes. The second approach is to have the design team ask questions to stakeholders (those with an interest in the dispute resolution system). The design team will need to determine who to ask, how to ask, and what questions to ask.

WHO TO CONSULT?

For any system of dispute resolution to be effective, the parties who have a vested interest in the system, or the "stakeholders," must agree to participate in the new system. Stakeholders could include employees, managers, lawyers, clients, customers, interest groups, and regulators. If stakeholders are not consulted, they may revert to their old ways and actively or passively refuse to implement or avoid the new processes. The more stakeholders are involved with and consulted on the design of the process, the greater the likelihood that the new system can be implemented with minimal disruption. The people to be consulted could include:

- those involved in the disputes,

- those affected by the outcome of disputes,

- those who may have disputes in the future,

- those who were involved in designing previous dispute resolution processes,

- those involved in governing the organization,

- those who may need to operate the system.

The most obvious group of people to involve are the current disputants and their advisors. These could include corporate executives who are involved in litigation, employees who have filed grievances, employees who have complained to management about working conditions, or the company's outside or in-house legal counsel. These people will be familiar with the types of disputes affecting the organization, and the difficulties with existing procedures. They will also be familiar with pressures on disputants that may affect their willingness to adopt new dispute resolution procedures.

The systems design team will also want to consult anticipated potential disputants and others who may operate within the new system. These may include people involved in making downsizing decisions, people who have significant contact with clients or customers, people who supervise employees, or people within the organization who may be asked to play a role in the new system (such as internal negotiators, mediators, arbitrators, investigators, or fact finders). Those who will use the new system will want to have input into decisions about processes that should be in place. Potential future disputants may also be able to be more objective than current disputants because their judgment may not be clouded by the emotion of a current dispute.

The system design team should also consult people who have been involved in the design of the current or prior dispute resolution systems since they may have insights into potential obstacles for the systems designers, such as warnings about those in the organization who may resist change. They may also be able to advise the design team about processes that have been attempted and rejected because they did not achieve the organization's objectives.

Others who are interested in the dispute resolution system should also be consulted. Public or quasi-public organizations are sometimes scrutinized by interest groups. If there are groups that perceive themselves as watchdogs of the organization for which the system is designed, those groups should be consulted to identify their views about the current dispute resolution system and possible areas of improvement. Often these groups offer valuable insights into the organization's operation.

It is also important to obtain input from those who govern the organization. These executives may provide the design team with insight into the culture of the organization. Perhaps more importantly, senior people in the organization can either facilitate the implementation of a new system or stall its progress. By obtaining their views and attempting to accommodate their needs, the systems design team can increase the likelihood that the new system will not be held up by those with authority.

HOW TO OBTAIN INFORMATION?

The ideal approach for the design team is to pose questions orally in a personal interview. People usually prefer this direct approach as they can present their views in a way that is interactive, friendly, and personal. Members of the systems design team will have the opportunity not only to hear what people have to say, but also to observe body language and listen to intonation. Sometimes, however, a personal interview is not possible, either because of the interviewees' unavailability or due to the distance between interviewer and interviewee. In those cases, interviews can be conducted by phone or in writing. Even where personal interviews are possible, some interviewees will ask to make written submissions to ensure that their views are considered by the entire ADR systems design team.

An interviewer must strike a delicate balance between conducting a thorough interview and respecting the fact that those being interviewed have tasks and priorities that are not necessarily associated with the dispute resolution processes. Interviewers should keep questions focused, structured, and precise to avoid burdening any individuals. Interviewees may appear to be open to spending a lot of time with the interviewer (so as not to appear opposed to a new dispute resolution system), but in reality, may resent the amount of time required of them. They may also fear that if they cut short the interview, their views will not be considered. It may, therefore, be helpful to review with the interviewee, in advance, the anticipated amount of time the interview will take to ensure the interviewee has the time available.

If interviewees are nervous or uncomfortable about personal interviews, the design team may want to send written questions to interviewees before the oral interview. The interview can still be free-flowing and need not be confined to the written questions.

Interviewees should be informed that the goal of the interview is not to gather information so that a system can be designed that will satisfy everyone; in fact, systems designers will usually receive conflicting advice and recommendations from stakeholders who have different needs and goals, and typically the systems design team will be unable to accommodate all of the stakeholders' concerns. Interviewees can be assured, however, that the systems design team will review and seriously consider all input.

If there is not enough time to conduct personal interviews, the design team may be able to hold an open meeting to obtain input from stakeholders.

When there are many stakeholders to interview, the design team may want to send questionnaires to stakeholders in order to obtain their perspectives. Some questions on the questionnaire should be quantitative and specific (such as asking on a scale of one to five, how satisfied the

respondent is with the current dispute resolution system).
Other questions should be qualitative and general (such as
why the respondent believes the current dispute resolution
system is not working).

At the end of this chapter is a sample of a questionnaire
that was used by the Law Society of Upper Canada for its
consultation with stakeholders relating to the design of an
ADR system. The Law Society was exploring how ADR
processes could be incorporated into its regulatory process
which dealt with, among other things, complaints about
the conduct of lawyers. This particular questionnaire was
sent to some representatives of the Canadian Bar Association and was designed to canvass their views on the issues
presented in the questionnaire.

Once the team has received responses to the questionnaires, it will need to analyze the responses to see
whether there is a pattern from which the team can draw
conclusions, and to see whether the respondents have
proposed any innovative ideas.

Questions that need to be asked in interviews or questionnaires will vary with each systems design project. A
list of possible questions is provided in the next two chapters. This list is not exhaustive; it is a guide intended to
raise some of the issues that may be important in the
design of a dispute resolution system.

Case Study: Bank of Montreal

The systems design team for the Bank of Montreal (BOM) included members of Stitt Feld Handy Houston, members of the BOM legal department, and a cross-section of BOM employees who would be responsible for implementing and administering the new system.

In retrospect, the design team did not do as detailed a diagnosis as it might have done. At the time, we did not fully appreciate the scope of diagnosis that was required. We did, however, speak individually with people at the BOM who were involved in dispute resolution. The design team included people in the bank who understood the bank's culture, goals, and limitations, and the other members of the design team relied heavily on their expertise. The design team also consulted representatives of small businesses to ascertain their views.

Case Study:
Ontario Human Rights Commission

The ADR systems design team for the Ontario Human Rights Commission included members of Stitt Feld Handy Houston, OHRC investigators, and senior OHRC staff who were responsible for designing and implementing the ADR system. The ADR systems design team was able to benefit from research performed on ADR

systems for other entities that investigated and adjudi-
cated complaints. For example, the team referred to a
study by Lisa Feld and Peter Simm of the use of ADR by
the College of Physicians and Surgeons of Ontario.

The design team conducted interviews with groups
that the Commission identified as stakeholders in the
system. The design team invited interest groups and
selected disputants' representatives from across the
province to discuss how the Commission should best
implement ADR. Each group spent an hour discussing
issues with the design team. The stakeholders who
were interviewed were invited to provide any written
material that they believed would be helpful to the
design team. Groups that were not offered an interview were invited to submit written material.

In order to focus the discussions in the interviews,
the design team sent out nine proposed topics for discussion before the interviews. Interviewees were free
to discuss these or any other topics relevant to the
design.

The design team limited the time for each interview
to one hour to accommodate as many groups as possible, to focus the discussions, and to ensure that the
interview did not monopolize the time of the people
who volunteered to participate in the interviews.

S U M M A R Y

DIAGNOSIS

- The ADR systems design team could include human resources personnel, senior executives, union representatives, members of the legal department, external consultants, and others.
- The team should include some of those employees who oppose the introduction of a new system.

ASK QUESTIONS TO

- current disputants
- future disputants
- other interested parties (e.g., interest groups)
- those with authority in the organization

QUESTIONS CAN BE POSED

- through personal interviews
- through telephone interviews
- at an open meeting
- through questionnaires

QUESTIONS SHOULD BE

- focused
- structured
- precise

QUESTIONNAIRE FOR STAKEHOLDERS
LAW SOCIETY OF UPPER CANADA

1. What goals do you believe that the Law Society regulatory process should be designed to achieve?

_____

_____

_____

_____

_____

2. Which type of problems do you think mediation would NOT be useful in resolving and why? (Indicate your choice by a check, you may check as many as you wish.)

❑ books and records
❑ borrowed from client
❑ breached/non-compliance with court order
❑ breached undertaking to LSUC
❑ breached undertaking to solicitor
❑ conflict/breach of fiduciary duty
❑ disputes between lawyers
❑ failed to co-operate with LSUC
❑ failed to file LSUC annual forms
❑ failed to honour financial obligation
❑ failed to reply
❑ failed to report/account
❑ failed to report to LPIC
❑ failed to serve client
❑ misappropriation
❑ mislead client/LSUC/etc.

❏ prepared false document
❏ practicing under suspension
❏ release of files/solicitors' lien
❏ sexual harassment
❏ other (specify) _____

Why?

_____

_____

_____

3. If mediation becomes part of the regulatory process,
    (check one):

❏ the mediator should hear from the disputants and then
   tell them what the answer should be (evaluative mediation).

OR

❏ the mediator should facilitate a discussion among the
   disputants (facilitative mediation).

4. In which of the following examples should the Law
    Society always participate as a party to mediation:

❏ books and records
❏ borrowed from client
❏ breached/non-compliance with court order
❏ breached undertaking to LSUC
❏ breached undertaking to solicitor
❏ conflict/breach of fiduciary duty
❏ disputes between lawyers
❏ failed to co-operate with LSUC

❑ failed to file LSUC annual forms
❑ failed to honour financial obligation
❑ failed to reply
❑ failed to report/account
❑ failed to report to LPIC
❑ failed to serve client
❑ misappropriation
❑ mislead client/LSUC/etc.
❑ prepared false document
❑ practicing under suspension
❑ release of files/solicitors' lien
❑ sexual harassment
❑ other (specify)

Why?   _____

_____

_____

_____

5. Do you think mediation should be voluntary for the
   lawyer, complainant, and the Law Society?

                yes   ❑   no   ❑

If no, then:

(a) if the complainant and lawyer want to mediate, should
    the Law Society be required to mediate?

                yes   ❑   no   ❑

(b) if the Law Society and the complainant want to medi-
    ate, should the lawyer be required to mediate?

                yes   ❑   no   ❑

(c) if the Law Society and the lawyer want to mediate,
should the complainant be required to mediate?

yes ❑   no ❑

6. *"If mediation becomes part of the regulatory process, the complainant must approve the settlement that is reached in mediation."*

Do you think this statement is true?

❑ always
❑ sometimes
❑ never

Please explain your response.

_____
_____
_____
_____
_____

7. If mediation becomes a part of the regulatory process,
what difficulties do you anticipate?

_____
_____
_____
_____
_____

8. How early in the regulatory process should mediation
   be used?

   _____

   _____

   _____

   _____

   _____

   _____

9. Please provide any other comments you may have
   about the possible use of mediation in the regulatory
   process.

   _____

   _____

   _____

   _____

   _____

CHAPTER 3

Diagnosis of the Organization

In order to recommend what processes will be needed to resolve disputes, the systems design team should understand organizational structure, culture, and goals. Team members can then design processes that are consistent with those goals. The team will likely have some familiarity with the organization, and interviews can fill in any gaps in knowledge. Some sample questions are as follows.

WHAT IS THE CULTURE OF THE ORGANIZATION?

Organizations, like societies, have cultures. If the systems design team recommends a process that runs contrary to the organizational culture, the recommendations are unlikely to be implemented by those who are familiar and comfortable with the existing culture. For this reason, the dispute resolution system must fit with the culture of the organization. For example, in some paramilitary organizations such as police forces, the prevalent view among those in positions of control is often influenced by the historical hierarchical governance of these organizations. Consequently, in these cases, a dispute resolution system that gives authority to disputants will feel foreign and is likely to be rejected both by those in control and by disputants who are comfortable with authoritative decision-making. In those situations, the design might focus on processes where decisions are made by those with authority (such as having a superior decide on the resolution of a dispute, or going to binding arbitration).

THE RCMP

Not all paramilitary organizations have a culture that supports authoritative decision-making to resolve disputes. The Royal Canadian Mounted Police, for example, has now incorporated consensual interest-based approaches to help resolve disputes among members of the force. This approach was only possible when the Chief of the RCMP, and others with power, publicly stated their support for consensual ADR processes.

The RCMP had to deal with such issues as the appropriate attire for a mediation, and whether disputants should address superior officers by rank in informal processes. In the end, they decided to adopt a flexible policy that allowed participants to dress and address others as they felt comfortable. Most mediations have proceeded with disputants not in uniform.

The design team may want to ask people within the organization about the existing culture, and those outside the organization about perceptions of the organization's culture. Specifically, questions about an organization's cul-ture can focus on the following issues:

- whether a hierarchical or egalitarian structure exists within the organization;

- how decisions are made;

- the level of autonomy given to employees;

- the employees' perceived and actual levels of dedication to the organization;

- the employee turnover rate;

- whether there is a code of expected conduct; and

- whether there are expected standards of behaviour for employees.

WHAT IS THE COMMUNICATION STRUCTURE IN THE ORGANIZATION?

Organizations have communication flows that allow people to access the information they need to perform their jobs effectively. Some organizations have formal structures of communication, using written memos or e-mail to communicate internally, while at others important information transfer occurs at the water cooler or at lunch. Some organizations have regularly scheduled and structured meetings, while others meet only when necessary. Some organizations have formal performance review processes for employees, while others do not.

The systems design team needs to understand the processes of communication and the lines of communication in order to assess the sources of conflict and determine the appropriate conflict resolution processes. By identifying how individuals in the organization obtain necessary information, the design team can become more familiar with the organization's communication structure.

The members of the design team who work at the organization can often supply the team with information about the communication flow. Interviews with other employees may provide anecdotal data about informal information flow.

The mandate of the design team usually does not call for a discussion or recommendations about communication patterns (though the team may want to report informally on its recommendations for improving communication). The team can use its understanding of the communication structure, however, to design a system better suited to the organization. The communication style of an organization is an important factor for the design team to consider when it is recommending appropriate ADR processes. For organizations where information is communicated mostly in writing, for example, the dispute resolution processes may need to produce a written solution to the dispute, so that appropriate information can be conveyed to those who need the information. Where the information flow is informal, however, the organization will likely be more amenable to informal and unstructured dispute resolution processes.

In some organizations, disputants may not feel free to communicate openly for fear of reprisal. They may also believe that it would be inappropriate to discuss certain issues unless their opinions are specifically canvassed. In those organizations, processes that require full and frank disclosure by disputants may be problematic since employees may be uncomfortable with those processes (unless the information and input can be received anonymously).

HOW TECHNOLOGICALLY ADVANCED IS THE ORGANIZATION?

As we move further into the computer age, some organizations try to remain on the technology frontier while others remain comfortable with technology that has historically served them well. The design team will want to explore the extent to which the organization it is diagnosing has embraced corporate technology, and integrated it into its existing process.

Information about the extent to which an organization uses new technology can be useful to the design team for two purposes. First, it can provide an insight into how quickly the organization likes to adapt to new circumstances and new processes. Organizations that reject new technology may be more resistant to innovative dispute resolution processes.

Second, when the employees in the organization are computer-literate and technologically advanced, the design team may be able to take advantage of the technology. For example, the organization may have the ability to track disputes, compile data about how the disputes are being resolved, and produce the information in a form that will allow the design team (or an external person who is assessing the system) to determine which processes are working effectively and how the system can be improved.

WHAT RESOURCES ARE AVAILABLE?

There is no purpose in designing a highly sophisticated and effective dispute resolution system if the system is simply too expensive or too time consuming for the organization to implement. Consequently, one of the main preliminary questions that needs to be asked of the senior people in the organization is, what financial and human resources are available to allocate to dispute resolution?

After all, dispute resolution systems, like most services and products, cost money. An organization will need to allocate resources to both systems design analysis itself and the implementation and operation of the system once it has been designed.

The amount of money needed to implement and generate the ADR system will depend on the system designed.

Simple systems that make use of the excess capacity of current employees (such as human resources and legal personnel) or re-allocate the job functions of existing employees may have minimal extra expense. Volunteer mediators (often inexperienced) may agree to provide some services to the organization to gain experience. A system need not be expensive to be effective. There may be some costs associated with educating and training employees to facilitate the operation of the system, but these costs can be controlled and spread out over time. Costs of training are discussed in Chapter 13.

Some organizations have budgeted hundreds of thousands of dollars (directly or indirectly) to deal with disputes, and money is no object to achieving the best system. Imperial Oil Limited is an example of a company that has allocated significant resources to ADR and the appropriate resolution of disputes. In most organizations, however, budgets limit the amount that can be spent on ADR systems designs and on the system itself.

ADR systems design consultants who assist with the design of the ADR system may charge $25,000 to $50,000 for the diagnosis and design of the system. Costs can be higher or lower, depending on the scope of the project and the sophistication of the system. The design process usually takes three to six months, though it could be completed in less time if necessary. If the company cannot afford to hire a consultant on a project basis it could choose instead to retain one on an hourly basis for advice. These individuals will usually charge $150 to $300 per hour for ADR systems design consulting work.

Once ADR processes are designed, people will be needed to manage them, to act as third-party neutrals in them, and to monitor and assess them. Even if funds are not available to pay outside people to perform these tasks, existing employees (such as human resources people) may be able to fill these roles.

For complicated ADR systems, the organization may need to retain external mediators and arbitrators. These experts typically charge $1,500 to $3,500 per day. In addition (or alternatively), the organization may need to hire as full-time employees mediators, ombudspeople, or others to allow the new system to operate. Salaries for mediators will range from about $25,000 to about $100,000.

If the budget does not allocate sufficient resources to dispute resolution, the design team may be able to use the money that it saves as a result of the implementation of more efficient processes; that is, the cost of implementing a system to more effectively resolve disputes must be weighed against the cost to an organization, both financial and otherwise, of leaving conflicts unresolved or resolving them less than effectively. Of course, the savings may be difficult to measure. Companies could try, however, to track the amount of time spent disputing and on dispute resolution, or survey general employee satisfaction. Although savings may not be directly traceable, an organization with an appropriate dispute resolution system and more satisfied employees may experience increased productivity and profit. In any event, it will be important for the design team to know its financial constraints before it designs its processes.

The challenge for the design team is to produce a structure that stays within the parameters set by the organization.

Case Study: Bank of Montreal

The Bank of Montreal wanted to integrate mediation into the process of resolving credit disputes between the bank and small business customers. When we looked at the corporate culture at the Bank of Montreal, we found an organization in transition. BOM, like other banks, had historically been a conservative organization with a hierarchical structure, where senior executives made all of the important decisions. Junior employees needed approval for all significant decisions. The BOM was attempting to shift its culture to become more user-friendly, so that customers would feel comfortable and enjoy dealing with the bank.

Community Banking Managers facilitated communication between customers and the bank, and senior executives received training in interest-based negotiation, in an attempt to reduce tension between the bank and its customers. The bank viewed mediation as another step to create goodwill between the bank and small businesses.

With respect to resources allocated to the ADR system, while the budget was not unlimited, the bank wanted to implement appropriate processes, even if they were more expensive than processes that were less effective.

Case Study:
Ontario Human Rights Commission

The Ontario Human Rights Commission had a huge caseload of human rights complaints, and was looking for a system that could assist with dispute resolution, without inhibiting the OHRC's mandate to protect the public interest. Commissioners were responsible for determining whether violations to the Ontario Human Rights Code had occurred, and the Commissioners delegated the responsibility of the day-to-day management of the OHRC to senior staff. Investigators across the province investigated alleged violations of human rights and assisted disputants in resolving issues before Commission hearings.

Investigators had significant autonomy to attempt to resolve disputes, though some settlements (if they involved actions to be performed in the future) needed the Commissioners' approval before taking effect.

Senior management regularly communicated with each other and discussed issues, attempting to reach a consensus rather than requiring a decision to be made.

Limited financial resources were available to the systems design team for the ADR system, and the OHRC did not want to increase costs significantly. Certain individuals could act as neutral mediators, though these individuals had been trained as investigators, not mediators.

S U M M A R Y

DIAGNOSIS OF THE ORGANIZATION

SAMPLE QUESTIONS:

- What is the culture (hierarchy, autonomy, decision making) of the organization?
- What is the communication structure in the organization?
- What financial and people resources are available for a dispute resolution system?

CHAPTER 4

Diagnosis of the Disputes

The systems design team will want to examine the nature of the disputes that the organization is having and expects to have. Armed with an understanding of the disputes, the design team can then structure processes that are well suited to resolve them. Although the design team will likely have some knowledge about current and expected disputes, questioning of stakeholders will likely be beneficial. Some sample questions are as follows:

IS THE ORGANIZATION'S GOAL TO RESOLVE INTERNAL OR EXTERNAL DISPUTES?

Sometimes organizations need ADR systems to deal with disputes they are having with other organizations (such as suppliers, creditors, or clients), while in other cases, organizations are more focused on internal disputes (such as disputes among members or employees of the organization).

For disputes between organizations, there may or may not be a continuing relationship. Where there is a relationship, it may not be one in which the disputants deal with each other on a daily basis. For internal disputes, the relationship between or among disputants can be a crucial element of the dispute, and employees may deal with each other on a daily basis.

For external disputes, if no agreement is reached, there could be expensive and protracted litigation. For internal disputes, if no agreement is reached, there could be stress, strife, and an unproductive work environment.

An organization's approach to internal and external disputes should not, however, be examined separately. How an organization resolves disputes with its employees can affect how others perceive the organization, and how others approach disputes that they may be having with the organization. If, for example, the organization encourages mediation and open, consensual approaches to resolving disputes internally, it will be more likely to convince other organizations to engage in consensual dispute resolution processes such as mediation for external disputes.

WHAT KINDS OF DISPUTES IS THE ORGANIZATION HAVING?

To develop an effective ADR plan, the dispute resolution systems design team will need to understand the types of disputes that the organization experiences.

Factual

Some disputes may be factual. In these cases, disputants may disagree about events, whether or not they are objectively determinable. For example, they may disagree about whether one person engaged in inappropriate behaviour (such as making a sexually explicit or a gender-insensitive remark); about whether an employee is working hard; or about whether an employee is stealing from the company.

If the organization experiences factual disputes, the systems design team may recommend a process to determine objective facts, either before or after a conflict arises. To achieve this, the design team may implement a process where the disputing parties can have access to someone who can assist them to determine facts, or perhaps make a decision with respect to the facts. It may be prudent to have an investigator or "fact finder" perform research and make recommendations based on an objective assessment of facts.

Technical

Systems designers may also encounter technical disputes. For example, scientists in a company may disagree about the correct formula for a new product; engineers in a company may disagree about the safest design for a building; or bookkeepers in a company may disagree about the proper accounting treatment of an expense for tax purposes. In those cases, the design team may recommend a system in which a neutral who is proficient in the technical area authoritatively resolves the technical dispute.

Technical disputes may have arisen because the technicians were not communicating with or presenting data to each other in a coherent or understandable way. In those cases, the organization may use formal communications mechanisms (such as memoranda) or mediation to assist the technicians to communicate more effectively.

Interpersonal

Interpersonal disputes can occur when people within an organization do not get along. Two individuals may have recurring but different disputes with each other, where, for example, each person perceives that the other is acting unreasonably. If an organization experiences many interpersonal disputes, the design team may recommend the use of interest-based mediation. Further, a reorganization or reallocation of tasks may be appropriate.

Legal

Legal disputes may also occur, perhaps about the interpretation of documents or agreements. For example, a dispute may arise about the interpretation of a collective
agreement or an employment contract. Legally trained
people within the organization can assist in resolving
these disputes relatively inexpensively, or lawyers or others outside the organization can provide guidance.

The systems design team should be aware, however,
that disputes that are presented as legal, could in fact be
factual or interpersonal. Employees may believe that if they
present a dispute in legal terms, they are more likely to
have the dispute resolved in their favour. For example, an
interpersonal dispute between employees who each
believe that they should get an office with a window could
be framed as a legal dispute concerning the benefits of
seniority in the organization. Moving behind the legal argument to the real issue can minimize the time and costs
associated with resolving the dispute.

Difference of Opinion

Another type of dispute that may be prevalent in organizations involves a difference of opinion about the future.
For example, employees may disagree about future demand
for the company's product or whether the company should

expand into a new market. For these kinds of disputes, interest-based processes such as negotiation and mediation may also be appropriate.

WHAT HAS BEEN TRIGGERING THE DISPUTES?

The design team will want to investigate what events trigger disputes. It would be a mistake to focus only on the conflict alone if there is a triggering event that can be controlled. Managing the triggering event and therefore the source of the disputes can significantly reduce the amount of conflict in an organization.

Disputes could be triggered, for example, by senior management making decisions that affect employees without consulting with employees (or their representative). In such cases, the systems design team could recommend a consultation process through which employees could have input into important decisions.

Another example of a triggering event could be the posting of the next week's work schedule by a manager each Friday. The dispute may manifest itself as a dispute about the type of work an employee is asked to do when the true source of the conflict could be the stress associated with the fact that the posting occurred on the Friday before the work was assigned. Arranging for an earlier posting could reduce stress and disputes about the type of work assigned.

HOW DOES THE COMPANY FIND OUT ABOUT DISPUTES?

In some organizations, there are formal processes for lodging complaints; in others, there is no formal process and disputes are dealt with when a manager learns of the dispute (either in a meeting or at the water cooler). The ADR systems design team will want to know how the organization learns about the dispute for two reasons. First, the organization may benefit from changing the process by which the organization learns of conflict. The existing process may be too cumbersome and formal, or too informal (so that conflict escalates while no one in authority knows that the conflict exists). The systems design team will need to examine whether the method by which the dispute comes to the attention of the organization is appropriate, and if not, what processes should be implemented so that an appropriate method exists.

Second, the organization will need to know how the organization learns about conflict so that it can determine when the new ADR processes should be triggered. The organization can provide disputants with the option (or requirement) to use the new processes only after the organization becomes aware that the conflict exists. The system that the design team establishes will need to provide processes that operate after the organization has learned of the conflict. For example, two employees may be having a dispute about whose desk should be located next to the window. The organization may have an ombudsperson who could deal with such relatively minor internal conflict. However, only after a manager learns of the dispute and recommends that the disputants see the ombudsperson can the dispute resolution model operate.

WHAT KINDS OF DISPUTES ARE LIKELY TO OCCUR IN THE FUTURE?

People will often predict that similar kinds of disputes will take place in the future as those that have occurred historically. Some organizations, however, can anticipate that new disputes are likely to occur in the future. For example, an organization that is changing its corporate culture from one where an authoritative president makes all major decisions to one where senior management shares in decision making, should anticipate disputes among managers concerning their new decision-making authority. Also, a company that is converting from wholesale selling to retail selling can anticipate a sharp increase in the number of customer complaints (if only because there are significantly more customers).

The design team should structure a system that can accommodate any anticipated changes in the pattern of disputes.

HOW MANY DISPUTES ARE THERE?

In some organizations, disputes are rampant; in others, they occur rarely but are significant when they do. The systems design team must determine the frequency of the disputes in order to recommend processes that can be implemented to deal with them.

If there are many disputes

There may be reasons why the disputes are so common and the systems design team can investigate why there are so many.

- The organization may be so large that people are continually confronting each other with issues, and therefore, disputes are inevitable;

- The senior people in the organization may believe that competition within the organization is a healthy component of a productive work environment, and the corporate culture therefore encourages conflict and confrontation;

- The significant conflict could result from a small number of antagonistic individuals;

- The volume of disputes may reflect unhappiness or uncertainty in the organization.

If there are many disputes, the design team could make recommendations to attempt to reduce the number of disputes. These recommendations may, however, be neither appropriate nor desirable. The amount of conflict may be a healthy sign of growth and development in the organization. If the conflict is dealt with efficiently and productively, the design team will want to consider whether the organization would benefit from a reduction in the amount of conflict. If the answer is no, the design team should focus on designing efficient dispute resolution processes. If the answer is yes, the design team should examine why disputes are arising and how to reduce the number of disputes.

Where disputes are common, the organization will need processes that are easily accessible and that can handle multiple disputes over a short period. These processes could include the ombudsperson model, mediation conducted by employee mediators, and supervisory decisions.

If there are few disputes

In other organizations, disputes will be rare. The goal of the systems design team would therefore usually be to identify how to deal with the conflict more effectively, rather than to determine how to reduce the number of disputes or why the disputes are occurring.

It may be that the organization has traditionally tolerated almost no disputes, and a small increase in the number and emotional tone of the disputes has caused those in control of the organization to search for a system to deal with the conflict. If that is the case, the systems design team may want to determine whether the new level of disputes is not only tolerable, but also healthy, and to investigate why the organization is unwilling to tolerate the level of disputes.

The disputes that are arising may be crippling the organization, both in terms of cost and emotional energy. If that is the case, the design team must ensure that the processes used to resolve the disputes are cost-effective and minimize any unnecessary negative emotion expended in the resolution of the dispute. Processes will need to be clear, accessible, and must reach a conclusion (have finality) within a reasonable period. Binding processes such as arbitration or having a superior decide could be available to disputants before significant time and energy are lost.

HOW MANY DISPUTANTS ARE THERE?

The ADR systems design team will need to assess how many people are involved in each type of dispute. If disputes involve two people, processes such as negotiation or simple mediation may be appropriate. If many individuals are involved in disputes, the organization may need to supply a facilitator who can ensure that appropriate communication is occurring among the group members, and that discussions lead productively toward resolution of issues.

ARE CERTAIN INDIVIDUALS COMMONLY INVOLVED IN DISPUTES?

Sometimes, although an organization has a relatively large number of disputes, the same individuals are involved in a significant percentage of the conflicts. This could occur as a result of the job functions of those individuals (where, for example, the individuals may be required to make unpopular decisions, or the individuals may be called upon when others are under stress); the individuals may be attempting to implement change and others are resistant to change; those individuals may be resistant to change; or the individuals may have personalities that make conflict inevitable.

In the first two cases (where conflict occurs as a result of the job function of the individuals or where individuals are attempting to implement unpopular change), the fact that certain individuals are involved in a large percentage of the conflict should not be viewed as a factor that needs to be addressed.

In either of the latter two cases (individuals are resistant to change or they have conflicting personalities), it may be appropriate for the systems design team to make recommendations that would minimize the interaction of these individuals with others in the organization. The team must be careful, however, to not engage in an exercise that is perceived to be critical of specific individuals if that is not within the team's mandate. The ADR design team may, however, recommend different reporting requirements or communication structures to minimize potentially hostile interactions.

HOW QUICKLY DO DISPUTES NEED TO BE RESOLVED?

Some disputes need to be resolved quickly in order to be beneficial. For example, the dispute could relate to an advertising decision that must be made by the end of the day. In such cases, the dispute resolution processes must take into account the urgency of resolution. As a result, the design team may recommend that other staff who can facilitate the resolution of the dispute (such as ombudspeople or mediators) be available on short notice. In addition (or alternatively), external people can be available on short notice.

Further, the design team may recommend short time frames for attempts at consensual resolution so that if the attempts are unsuccessful, final decisions can be made promptly.

For other disputes, there may be less urgency in reaching a decision. These types of disputes could relate to, for example, strategic-planning decisions. The dispute resolution processes can therefore take more time when needed.

ARE THE DISPUTES CYCLICAL?

In most organizations, conflicts occur at random times, and there is no way to predict when and how disputes will arise. In other organizations, however, there is a cyclical nature to the disputes. For example, disputes may arise at a certain time of year, when tensions are high and there is a lot of organizational activity. There may be particular periods of time in a cycle when everyone is under stress and working harder. The design team will need to provide processes that are available when they are needed, recognizing any cyclical nature of the disputes.

SETTING CROP PRICES

For example, the Ontario Farm Products Marketing Commission regulates the setting of prices for vegetable crops sold to vegetable processors in Ontario by, among other things, setting out dispute resolution procedures for disputes between the Vegetable Growers Marketing Board (representing crop growers) and the crop processors. The negotiations concerning price and terms of sale occur in the winter, and disputes arise when the parties are unable to resolve

issues at these negotiations. The ADR process they
have developed has independent mediators and arbitrators available in the winter, when disputes are
likely to arise. There is no need for a dispute resolution system to be in place for the balance of the year,
as disputes rarely occur. The two groups meet with a
facilitator in the summer to discuss issues of common
interest and to plan the dispute resolution processes
for the upcoming winter.

IS RELATIONSHIP IMPORTANT TO THE DISPUTING PARTIES?

Sometimes one-time disputes occur in which the disputants will never have contact with each other again after
their issue has been resolved. For example, people working in a large company in different cities on a unique project may not have future contact. Similarly, two companies
that do not deal with each other on a regular basis may
find themselves in a dispute.

In such cases, the disputants are more concerned that
the dispute is resolved, than that the dispute is resolved in
a way that preserves the disputants' ability to work
together in the future. As a result, the design team may
recommend quick methods of determining rights (such as
arbitration) once all necessary facts have been established.

The more common situation, however, occurs where the
disputants will have dealings with each other after the dispute
has been resolved. Examples could include two employees
of a company having a dispute, or two companies, a supplier

and a retailer, disputing the terms of sale of some supplies. In these cases, the processes used to resolve the disputes should not leave the disputants angry with each other about the dispute or the process for resolving it. Processes should also provide disputants with a framework for resolving future disputes themselves. Interest-based negotiation or mediation may therefore be appropriate in such cases.

The design team should be aware that some disputants may assume too quickly that their dispute is one where relationship is irrelevant. Disputes between two people in an organization, even where the people believe they will not have further contact, may fall into this category. People in an organization, even a large one, usually find that they interact again after the dispute is resolved. The same can also be true for disputes between people in the same industry, but in different organizations. The safer assumption is that relationship is important, unless it is clear that the individuals will have no further dealings with each other.

IS PRECEDENT IMPORTANT?

Regardless of whether the disputants will have contact with each other in the future, the systems design team will need to determine whether the substantive result of disputes should be recorded so that the information can be used in future similar situations, either to prevent disputes or to resolve them.

In litigation, reasons given in cases (or precedents) are used by judges to help them resolve similar cases when they arise. They are also used by lawyers to predict the outcomes of disputes or to assess the risk of a particular course of action.

Within organizations, where disputes of a similar nature continually arise, resolution of conflict in a particular situation can be used to resolve a future dispute. Those organizations will want to keep track of the resolution of disputes and make these results available to future disputants and dispute resolvers.

In other organizations, where disputes always raise different issues, there is less concern about precedent and consequently less need to record the results of disputes.

IS CONFIDENTIALITY IMPORTANT?

For some disputes, the dispute itself, the identity of the disputants, and any resolution of the dispute must be kept confidential. This may be necessary to protect the disputants' reputations, to avoid embarrassment, or to avoid disclosure of trade secrets to competition. For example, where there is an allegation of sexual harassment, the stigma associated with the accusation, even if it is without merit, could remain with the alleged harasser; alternatively, the complainant may wish to maintain confidentiality. Another example may arise also, if there is a dispute between organizations about patent infringements, the two disputing organizations may want the details of the formula (and thus the dispute) kept confidential from competitors.

It may therefore be necessary to devise processes to protect the confidentiality of information. This can be done, for example, by having those involved in dispute resolution sign confidentiality agreements and perhaps by requiring them to destroy any notes taken in the process of dispute resolution.

For some disputes, such as those involving allegations of sexual harassment, the identities of the disputants may remain confidential, but the nature of the dispute and its resolution can be disclosed. In those cases, anonymous summaries of the disputes could be published and disseminated.

There are other types of disputes where the identities of the disputants need not be kept confidential, but the nature of the dispute and any resolution of it must be kept confidential. A family fighting over control of a family business is one such example. In those situations, binding arbitration may be appropriate so that the dispute resolution process remains confidential.

Where there is a concern about confidentiality, it is more difficult to use the precedential value of the resolution of the dispute. Organizations may be forced to balance the desire for precedents with the need for confidentiality.

ANONYMOUS REPORTS

The College of Physicians and Surgeons of Ontario handles disputes about the conduct of physicians. The College has developed a mediation process to resolve complaints. For good reason, physicians are concerned about their reputations and want a confidential process. However, the College needs to keep its members informed about any resolutions to disputes arising from allegations of inappropriate conduct.

If disputes are resolved in mediation, the College publishes anonymous summaries in a members' newsletter. Members are therefore informed of resolutions while the confidentiality of the identity of the physician and complainant are preserved. Where the resolution involves a public reprimand or apology, summaries need not be anonymous.

Case Study: Bank of Montreal

The Bank of Montreal was focused on disputes with its small business customers, specifically concerning the bank's decision to reduce or eliminate existing credit. Most of the disputes were factual or interpersonal, and occurred because the small business was unable to satisfy its financial obligations to the bank, and perceived the bank's decision to reduce or eliminate credit as arbitrary and unreasonable. The bank anticipated that these types of disputes would recur in the future. The disputes did not need to be resolved urgently, except when the small business had an urgent need for cash.

It was difficult to determine the number and frequency of the disputes. Although few customers used the bank's existing dispute resolution channels, this was not because there were a limited number of disputes; rather, it appeared that many customers became frustrated and approached other banks for credit rather than use the BOM's existing dispute resolution processes.

There did not seem to be any factor that could be used to predict the timing of disputes (they were not cyclical), and no employees were continually involved in disputes with customers (other than the Community Banking Managers, who were responsible for dealing with the disputes).

Once a dispute was resolved, a continuing relationship was likely to occur between the customer and the bank. Even if the relationship ended (if credit were revoked), the bank was concerned about its reputation and did not wish to be perceived as having acted unreasonably.

Precedent was not particularly important to either the bank or the customer, as the credit difficulties were perceived to be unique situations with potentially unique solutions. Confidentiality was sometimes a concern, either for the bank or the customer, depending on the solution adopted. The bank, however, wanted to promote the fact that it offered innovative dispute resolution options so that it could enhance its reputation and attract new customers.

Case Study:
Ontario Human Rights Commission

The Ontario Human Rights Commission is focused generally on reducing discrimination in Ontario, and specifically with rectifying violations of the Ontario Human Rights Code. If there were a perceived violation of human rights, the aggrieved party could file a complaint with the OHRC. The disputes were usually factual and legal, and often interpersonal.

The OHRC dealt with many disputes every year, and the disputes were not cyclical. Parties to the dispute included the complainant, individual respondents, and organizational respondents (such as companies that were alleged to have systemically violated human rights). Advocacy groups participated when requested, but were not officially involved in the complaints process unless they represented one of the disputants.

Some companies (or organizations) had many complaints lodged against them, either because they were large or because they engaged in discriminatory practices, while other organizations had single complaints lodged against them.

Although there was no urgency in resolving disputes, the OHRC did not want new processes to delay a hearing before the Commission, if such a hearing were ultimately necessary. Any new process, such as mediation, would need to take place at a time when it did not slow the investigation or hearing process.

The disputing parties often had a significant stake in enhancing (or at least preserving) their relationship. Disputants commonly had ongoing business or working relationships, and often resided in the same community.

Both confidentiality and precedent were important to disputants. Confidentiality was important for disputants to protect their reputations, and precedent and publicity were important to the OHRC to demonstrate that it was fulfilling its legislative mandate to protect the public interest.

S U M M A R Y

DIAGNOSING THE DISPUTES

SAMPLE QUESTIONS:

- Is the organization's focus on internal or external disputes, or both?

- What kinds of disputes is the organization having (factual, technical, legal, interpersonal)?

- What causes the disputes?

- What kinds of disputes are likely to occur in the future?

- How many disputes are there?

- How many disputants are there (one on one, groups)?

- How quickly do disputes need to be resolved?

- Are certain individuals commonly involved in disputes?

- Are disputes cyclical?

- Is relationship important to the disputing parties?

- Is precedent important (will similar disputes arise in the future)?

- Is confidentiality important?

CHAPTER 5

Dispute Resolution Requirements

The systems design team will need to understand the existing dispute resolution processes, and the constraints that the organization faces in implementing a new ADR system. The design team must also be careful not to overstep its mandate for designing the system.

WHAT IS THE MANDATE OF THE DESIGN TEAM?

When organizations decide to review the way they resolve disputes, that does not necessarily mean that the organization has decided to completely reassess everything it does. Generally, systems design specialists are asked to redesign specific aspects of the dispute resolution process of the organization, not the entire process.

LIMITS PLACED ON THE DESIGN TEAM

For one systems design project in which we participated, the organization wanted a system to deal with complaints about some of its members. The organization received various complaints about the conduct of its members and wanted a system to deal fairly with concerns that were raised. Some complaints related to alleged inappropriate sexual behaviour by some of the members, while other complaints related to other alleged inappropriate behaviour. Senior management specifically instructed the design team not to design a system to deal with complaints relating to inappropriate sexual behaviour.

WHAT PROCESSES HAVE BEEN USED TO RESOLVE DISPUTES IN THE PAST?

The design team will need to ascertain which aspects of the system are working effectively, and which processes need to be changed. Processes should be preserved if they assist in the resolution of disputes, provide timely and cost-effective solutions, and satisfy organizational goals.

Understanding the existing dispute resolution mechanisms will assist the systems design team to determine why problems may be occurring. The team will want to examine why the current structures are not meeting the organization's objectives. For example, if the organization is attempting to reduce costs, the design team would need to determine whether the cost of the current system is adequately controlled. Or, if the organization is concerned about reducing the time needed to resolve conflict, the team would need to determine whether the processes used are efficient.

It would be helpful to determine whether the organization had experimented with dispute resolution processes that were rejected. Understanding previously failed attempts at ADR systems design may help the ADR design team to predict which processes will work in the future.

PRESERVING ASSETS

Sometimes a conflict arises in which the disputants are fighting over assets that are losing their value over time. If the disputants leave the assets alone, they may lose some or all of their value by the time the dispute is resolved. For example, a dispute may involve the ownership of fruit. If the fruit dispute is not resolved immediately, the fruit will perish and become worthless.

Similarly, a dispute in an organization may revolve around how cash should be invested. During the dispute, if no investment is made, interest will not be earned. In these situations, the organization may need a system that offers safeguards to maintain the assets (as much as possible) while the dispute is being resolved. The fruit, for example, could be sold and the money put into trust pending resolution of the dispute. Similarly, the cash could be invested safely in a bank while the dispute is resolved concerning its long-term investment.

SHOULD EXTERNAL OR INTERNAL PEOPLE BE USED TO HELP RESOLVE THE DISPUTES?

If the proposed ADR processes require the use of neutrals (for example, mediators or arbitrators), the design team must assess whether to use the organization's employees (current or future) or professional neutrals.

Obviously, using staff is usually less expensive than retaining outside expertise. Human resources staff or ombudspeople may agree to act as neutrals exclusively, or may do so as part of their job function. Internal people are also familiar with the operation of the organization and may have expertise concerning the issues in dispute. They may also be respected by the disputants.

On the other hand, external neutrals may have the experience and training required to resolve disputes, whereas employees may not be as familiar with the dispute resolution process. Furthermore, external people may possess the independence necessary to gain the disputants' trust, who may not perceive other employees as neutral, impartial, or objective.

Case Study: Bank of Montreal

The design team for the Bank of Montreal was asked to create a process for resolving only credit disputes between the bank and its small business customers. The bank wanted to implement ADR in this limited context before determining whether it should introduce the system to deal with other disputes in the organization.

The existing BOM process for dealing with credit disputes between the bank and its small business customers was as follows: first, the small business person and the bank manager would attempt to resolve the dispute. If no agreement was reached, the business person could negotiate with the regional Community Banking Manager. If the conflict was still unresolved, the business person could appeal to the office of the Vice-Chairman.

The bank retained the ultimate decision about whether to reduce or eliminate credit if the customer was in breach of the credit agreement, and wanted to maintain this authority.

The BOM was concerned that during the dispute resolution process, there existed a possibility that small business owners may attempt to sell or further encumber assets on which credit was granted, and asked the design team to address this issue.

With respect to whether the bank preferred internal or external neutrals, the bank believed that it was important for business people to be confident that the mediators were neutral and that the bank was making a real attempt to resolve the conflict. The bank therefore preferred using external mediators.

Case Study:
Ontario Human Rights Commission

The Ontario Human Rights Commission wanted to implement appropriate ADR processes just after a complaint had been filed, in the hope of providing effective early resolution where possible. Any process needed to be concluded within 90 days of the filing of the complaint, and had to be consistent with the OHRC's mandate to protect the public interest.

Under the existing scheme, OHRC investigators researched the complaints and then attempted to persuade disputants to reach an agreement that was satisfactory to both them and the OHRC. If no agreement were reached, a Commission hearing would determine whether there had been discrimination, and the appropriate remedy.

To save costs, the OHRC wanted to use its internal staff wherever possible.

S U M M A R Y

DIAGNOSIS OF
DISPUTE RESOLUTION REQUIREMENTS

SAMPLE QUESTIONS:

- What is the scope of the ADR system to be designed?

- What processes have been used in the past?
  - how well have they worked?
  - what elements can be improved?

- Do certain steps that need to be taken during the dispute resolution process (e.g., to ensure preservation of assets)?

- Should external or internal people help to resolve the disputes?
  - look at cost, experience, training, and independence of individuals

CHAPTER 6

Interests

Once the systems design team has gathered its information, it will be in a position to design the system and implement processes that will help the organization achieve its goals.

The design team should examine the appropriateness of the different ADR processes, and then recommend which process or processes best meet organizational objectives. For many types of disputes, the disputants should first attempt a brief relationship-building process, and if that does not resolve the disputes, they can use a process that will provide a final decision.

As Ury, Brett, and Goldberg discussed in *Getting Disputes Resolved* (1988), there are three approaches to resolving disputes: a power-based approach, a rights-based approach, and an interest-based approach.

POWER AND RIGHTS

Disputants may be tempted to resort to power before considering other options for resolving a conflict. Power is used to influence the behaviour of others by forcing them to make choices according to the will of the person with power. A weaker person has the perception that the powerful person can cause adverse consequences if the weaker person does not accede to the will of the stronger.

Although the use of power sometimes achieves its desired end, it has drawbacks. After the dispute, a person on whom power has been exerted may be angry, and the relationship between the disputants may be irreparably harmed. As a result, the weaker disputant may resist implementing a solution that has been achieved through the exertion of power, and may seek opportunities for revenge. Furthermore, the use of power by one person may cause the other person to use power, and the ensuing battle may not be the most effective approach to conflict resolution for either disputant.

An alternative to the use of power is adopting a rights-based approach. In a rights-based process, someone other than the disputants decides who is right and how the conflict should be settled. Litigation and arbitration are examples of rights-based processes. Although one of the disputants may be vindicated by rights-based processes, the disputants may not be best served by using one as a first step in dispute resolution.

Since there will be a winner and a loser in rights-based processes, the loser may disagree with the result, harbour resentment, and be unwilling to implement the decision. Since disputants have limited control over the criteria that someone else considers appropriate when making a rights-based determination, at least one of the parties may not perceive the solution as fair. Furthermore, relationships may be damaged or even destroyed in the process of finding a rights-based solution, as with the use of power. Also, the disputants are unlikely to have the opportunity to speak directly to each other and vent frustrations. Rights-based processes are discussed in more detail in Chapter 9.

WHAT ARE INTERESTS?

Interest-based processes for dispute resolution focus on the disputants' interests rather than their rights or their power. Peoples' interests are their goals, wants, or needs. They are the reasons behind the positions that the people are advocating. Interests can be satisfied in a number of ways; positions can be satisfied in only one way.

Negotiation and mediation are the two most common interest-based processes used by organizations. Negotiation and mediation are discussed in Chapters 7 and 8.

Interest-based processes are consensual and therefore the conflict will only be resolved if all of the disputants agree to the solution. In an interest-based solution, there is neither a winner nor a loser, and the disputants try to persuade each other, not third parties, about the merits of their case.

Perhaps the best way to illustrate the difference between positions and interests is to relate an example from a student who had completed one of our ADR Workshops, and learned the difference between interests and positions.

WHERE TO GO FOR DINNER?

A woman was in the car with her husband and nine-year-old son and were debating where to go for dinner. Her son insisted that they go to an Indian food restaurant, while her husband was adamant that he preferred chicken. Her son argued that it was his turn to decide where to go for dinner. Her husband argued that since he was paying, he was entitled to decide.

Both individuals were putting forward positions and arguments about why their position was correct. The woman decided to convert the process from a rights-based to an interest-based approach to problem solving. To ascertain her husband's interests, she asked her husband why he wanted to go to the chicken restaurant. He said that he did not want to pay the high prices at the Indian food restaurant and, in addition, Indian food upset his stomach.

She then asked her son why he wanted to go to the Indian food restaurant. He responded that the Indian food restaurant was located next to one of his favourite toy stores, and that he wanted the opportunity to buy a toy.

Once the interests were uncovered, the father and son could see a resolution that satisfied both of their interests, and weren't forced to choose one position over the other. The family agreed to go to the chicken restaurant for dinner and stop at the toy store later. The option satisfied the interests of both the father and the son, and was achieved without determining who was right and who was wrong.

Interest-based approaches to dispute resolution assist people with seemingly unreconcilable positions to find options that satisfy their interests.

WHY USE INTEREST-BASED APPROACHES FIRST?

When designing an ADR system for an organization, the design team should usually recommend that disputing parties use interest-based approaches before they resort to rights-based or power-based approaches. When solutions are based on disputants' interests rather than their rights, the disputants are more likely to be satisfied with the result, and therefore more willing to implement it and abide by its terms.

Also, if disputants resolve conflict through interest-based processes, they may be able to improve rather than destroy their relationship. In addition, an interest-based process provides disputants with a framework that they can use in the future to deal with unanticipated disputes. Further, interest-based processes can yield creative, elegant, and often unanticipated solutions to seemingly unsolvable problems. Finally, interest-based approaches leave disputants with control over their own destinies, rather than delegating that control to a third party.

THE FLOODING HOME

A couple bought a home from a farmer. Unfortunately, the land around the house flooded every spring. The couple sued the farmer and the municipality (the latter for not providing appropriate drainage). Both the farmer and the municipality claimed that they were not responsible. Rights-based settlement discussions did not resolve the conflict, so the disputants retained an interest-based mediator.

Instead of focusing on the issue of compensation, the mediator focused on the couple's interests: a comfortable home that did not flood. The mediator also learned that the farmer had extra top soil from his farm.

The parties crafted a solution where the farmer would provide top soil, and the municipality provided machinery to allow the couple to smooth the top soil on the land to avoid future flooding. No one had to admit fault or wrongdoing, and all of the disputants were satisfied with the result.

Interest-based approaches to dispute resolution do not always lead to a settlement of the dispute, since disputants will have to agree on any solution to the conflict. If interest-based approaches are used first, and if they do not yield a settlement, the disputants can then resort to a rights-based process. If a rights-based process is used first, it will yield a solution and never allow for the opportunity to try for more satisfactory interest-based solutions.

S U M M A R Y

INTERESTS

- use interest-based approaches before rights-based or power-based approaches

- interests are the goals, wants, or needs, behind the positions

- interests can be satisfied a number of ways

- interest-based approaches include negotiation, mediation, and the ombudsperson

CHAPTER 7

Interest-Based Negotiation

The most basic and common interest-based process for resolving disputes is interest-based negotiation or principled negotiation, which was first presented in the classic book *Getting to Yes*, (1992).

In a principled negotiation, the disputing parties meet with each other, without the assistance of a third-party neutral, and attempt to determine each other's interests and generate options that satisfy the interests of all parties. This approach to negotiating, unlike some other schools of negotiating, does not prescribe what the negotiator should say at every point in the negotiation. It is a framework that allows its proponents consistently to achieve good results.

THE SEVEN ELEMENTS
OF PRINCIPLED NEGOTIATION

The seven elements of principled negotiation developed by Roger Fisher and discussed in *Beyond Machiavelli* (1994) and *Getting Ready to Negotiate* (1994) are as follows:

1. Alternatives

Before entering into a negotiation, each disputant must determine what she or he will do if an agreement cannot be reached. That is, the disputant must consider the "alternatives." Although this term usually connotes choices or options, in principled negotiation it refers to the courses of action that a negotiator can follow, regardless of the desires of the other negotiator, and without the other negotiator's consent.

Principled negotiation suggests that each disputant consider all of his or her alternatives and identify the best one. This is known as the "Best Alternative To a Negotiated Agreement" or "BATNA." Having numerous alternatives can give a disputant a false sense of security. The disputant can only choose one course of action if the negotiation does not resolve the dispute, and cannot act on the others.

Each disputant should make his or her BATNA as real and as concrete as possible, and not leave it as hypothetical. Developing a BATNA, therefore, may require some research prior to the negotiation.

Once the BATNA is concrete, the negotiator should see if it can be improved. Improving a BATNA is a classic way to increase negotiating power. By making the BATNA concrete and as good as it can possibly be, the disputant can enter the negotiation with a clear understanding of what is the best thing he or she can do if the principled negotiation breaks down.

Once the disputants know their respective BATNAs, they should put them away, and not use them during the negotiation process. At the end of the negotiation, the BATNA can be used to measure whether a deal proposed by the other person is better or worse than walking away from the table. The other six elements should govern a disputant's actions in the negotiation.

Sometimes disputants make the mistake of rejecting a proposal and then find out that their BATNA is worse than the proposal they rejected. At the end of a negotiation, negotiators should accept a proposal if it is better than their BATNA (even if they believe the proposal is not objectively reasonable). Similarly, if all potential resolutions to a dispute are worse than the disputants' BATNA, the negotiator should reject these potential resolutions, even if the disputants have invested a lot of time and effort in the negotiation. There is no shame in not reaching a deal in a negotiation.

Every negotiation will therefore be a success if the disputants achieve a deal that is better than their respective BATNAs. They will have accomplished together what they could not do separately. Similarly, a negotiation may be a success even if an agreement is not reached if the disputants have explored all possible resolutions and realize that the best outcome is achieved by proceeding independently.

Every disputant in a negotiation has a BATNA, though the BATNA may not always be good. At times, all of a person's alternatives may be unattractive, but one of the alternative courses of action will still be the best.

BATNAs should be realistic, but not overly optimistic. When two employees in an organization have a dispute, their BATNAs may be to proceed to a rights-based process if they cannot resolve their disputes in the negotiation. At the rights-based process (such as a binding hearing with an arbitrator), there are risks that the decision may not be to either disputant's satisfaction. Therefore, each employee's BATNA should not be to "win an arbitration" because that result can never be guaranteed. The BATNA in such cases may be to "go to arbitration with a 50 percent likelihood of success, according to my lawyer."

2. Interests

In a principled or interest-based negotiation, the disputing parties focus on interests not positions. As discussed in Chapter 6, interests are the disputants' wants, needs, and desires, and can be satisfied in a number of ways, whereas positions can only be satisfied one way.

Sometimes people who are involved in negotiations are not upfront with their interests because they believe they are better off hiding them. In these cases, negotiators need to ask open questions (which cannot be answered with "yes" or "no"), in an attempt to explore the other person's true interests. Asking why the person is advocating a particular position (what they hope to achieve) can be an effective way to uncover interests. Or, a probing negotiator may propose a number of options for resolving the conflict, and ask why each option is not viable as a solution to the problem. Based on the answers, the negotiator may be able to discern the other person's interests.

3. Options

After identifying the interests of both parties, the disputants can generate options that attempt to satisfy these interests. The disputants' goal should be to generate as many and as creative options as possible. Options, unlike alternatives, are the possible solutions that the disputing parties can implement with each other's consent and cooperation.

One way to generate options is to brainstorm and freely create options. Brainstorming is most effective if the disputants follow two basic ground rules: The first rule is that options are not offers and they can be presented without commitment from the presenter. Options cannot be accepted or rejected. Disputants can therefore feel free to brainstorm options that they are not necessarily prepared to propose as offers. Second, neither party should criticize options as they are being generated. If disputants can generate options without of fear of criticism, they are more likely to offer creative suggestions.

It is important to remember that options that may appear to be unworkable could later lead to viable options. The purpose of the ground rules is to facilitate creativity and permit the parties to generate as many options as possible even if they appear initially to be unfeasible.

EMPLOYEES COMPETE WITH EMPLOYER

An employer was suing its former employees for leaving their employment with confidential documents, customer lists, and pricing information, and for going into competition with the employer (breaching their "fiduciary duties"). The employees counterclaimed against the employer for slander.

One of the options proposed by the employer in the settlement negotiation was that the employees could return to work for the employer. Obviously, neither the employer nor the employees wanted to proceed with this option and they were both anxious to criticize it and explain why it was unworkable. This option, however, led to other options, including the option that the employees agree to buy a certain amount of product from the employer over a certain period, and sell the product in new markets that the employees had developed. This option was eventually fine-tuned and accepted by the employer and employees. With this solution, the employees had access to products that they would not otherwise have had, and the employer had guaranteed revenue and the ability to sell the products into new markets. The solution had been developed from what initially appeared to be a ridiculous and unworkable option.

Unfortunately, disputants often become fixated on their positions and are hesitant to generate options that differ from their positions. If, however, they can put aside the issue of who is right and who is wrong, and focus instead on options that may satisfy their interests, they may be able to overcome their differences and craft a solution.

4. Legitimacy

After the options are generated, the disputants must choose among them. They will be searching for a solution that is fair to them, and that the other disputants will be prepared to accept. To assist them, and to protect them from being taken advantage of, disputants can refer to legitimate standards or objective criteria such as precedents, benchmarks, and similar disputes in other contexts. By referring to external standards rather than focusing on power and coercion, the disputants can be confident that the solution will be objectively fair.

HOW MUCH IS THE RENT?

Disputants may be able to agree to be bound by a particular external standard, even where they do not know the consequences of agreeing to the standard. For example, in a dispute concerning the appropriate rent to be paid by a tenant to a landlord, both disputants agreed to be bound by the opinion of a particular real estate expert. This agreement was reached despite the fact that neither disputant knew the rent that the real estate expert would determine to be fair.

Principled negotiators are open to persuasion when presented with objective standards, even if they had not considered those standards. When disputants demonstrate that they are open to persuasion (though not coercion), they are more likely to be persuasive.

Relying on objective, legitimate benchmarks protects disputants from exploitation by aggressive bargainers. Since objective standards are inherently fair, insisting on objective criteria is equivalent to insisting on fairness.

5. Communication

All negotiation involves communication. A communication breakdown may, in fact, have caused the conflict in the first place. If the disputants can focus on *how* they communicate (in addition to *what* they say), they will be more likely to resolve their dispute.

AND, NOT BUT

Sometimes, changing one word in a sentence can completely change the perception that the other person has, while leaving the point of the sentence intact. For example, the word "but" is sometimes called "the great eraser" since its use erases any productive comments that preceded it. For example, in the statement, "You make a good point, but we must look forward, not backward," the "but" erases the benefit of the recognition of a good point. Use of the word "and" instead of "but" can significantly decrease antagonism and increase the likelihood that the other person will be receptive to suggestions. The statement would then be, "You have made some good points and we have to look forward knowing that."

Communication involves both speaking and listening, and knowing how to listen well can mean the difference between being persuasive and understood, and being mis-understood. Active listening is one of the most effective techniques in a negotiator's repertoire. Despite its name, active listening involves not only listening. In fact, the major component of active listening is paraphrasing or restating what the other person has just said. Paraphrasing may begin with "If I understand you correctly..." or "You appear to be saying...", followed by a summary of the points the other person has just made.

Paraphrasing should not be used sarcastically, and the speaker should paraphrase as accurately as possible. The purpose of paraphrasing is not to have the other person see the error of his or her ways, but rather, to understand what the other person is saying, and to demonstrate that understanding to the speaker.

Although paraphrasing sounds easy, it is one of the most difficult techniques in negotiation. It is especially difficult where the other negotiator has said something that the listener vehemently disagrees with. Our natural tendency is to argue and to tell the person why they are wrong, rather than attempt to understand.

Paraphrasing does not mean agreeing with what has been said; rather, it is an attempt to understand, and to demon-strate that understanding to the other person. People who feel heard and understood are more likely to listen to and attempt to understand the concerns of others.

Paraphrasing offers three main benefits:

1. The listener may have the facts wrong. By paraphrasing, facts can be clarified and perceptions corrected.

2. Paraphrasing will stop a cycle of repetition that will typically stall a negotiation. When a person does not feel understood, that person may repeat his or her point, usually in an angrier and louder tone, in order to be understood. Paraphrasing eliminates the need for this repetition, as the person will know that his or her point has been heard and understood.

3. People like to hear their own arguments. They think that their arguments are good ones, and they enjoy hearing them. Therefore, paraphrasing may improve the relationship of the disputants by conveying respect and a desire to understand the other person's perspective.

Although paraphrasing is a key tenet of active listening, it is only one component of the process. Active listening can include asking clarifying questions, determining underlying values, and acknowledging emotions.

6. Relationship

In most negotiations, people have a relationship that extends beyond the particular dispute, and they would be better served if they negotiate in a way that maintains or improves rather than destroys their relationship.

One method of improving the relationship during negotiation is to separate the people from the problem, and to be soft on the people, but hard on the problem. This does not mean, however, that a negotiator can ignore people issues and focus only on the substantive issues. Certainly, the people issues need to be addressed. The negotiator can try to find out concerns that the other person has, take breaks when appropriate, and address, in a positive way, any emotional issues that arise. By separating the people from the problem, a principled negotiator can improve rather than destroy the relationship during the negotiation.

NEGOTIATION JUJITSU

When a negotiator is confronted with someone who attacks the negotiator personally, the negotiator can play negotiation jujitsu, and deflect that attack onto the problem. Negotiation Jujitsu is discussed in *Getting to Yes* (1992). If, for example, one disputant says to another, "You don't know anything about how this organization operates. You're ignorant. You've only been here two months and I've been here for 15 years," the recipient of the personal attack might be tempted to defend him or herself, discuss credentials, counter-attack, and criticize the other person personally. Instead, the recipient of the personal attack could deflect the attack onto the problem by saying, "As someone who understands this organization, you must have some ideas about how this issue has been resolved in the past. What has been done in similar disputes in the past?" By deflecting the attack and refocusing on the problem, the individual has chosen not to participate in what could have been a damaging spiral of escalating personal attacks.

7. Commitment

Logically, negotiators should only commit to a resolution at the end of a negotiation, after they have examined all of the options. In practice, however, many people commit at the beginning of the negotiation, before they know all of the facts. Stating an initial position is one such example. Negotiators often commit to a position and change their commitment during the negotiation process. Ideally, commitment is left until the end of the process, after negotiators have discovered each other's interests and generated options.

Negotiators can be open to persuasion, open to creative options and new ideas, and soft on the other person without being weak bargainers. They protect themselves by not committing until the end.

Before committing, negotiators should review their BATNAs to determine whether the option proposed is better or worse than the BATNA. In this way, the negotiators will know whether to commit or walk away from the negotiating table.

INCORPORATING PRINCIPLED NEGOTIATION INTO THE ADR SYSTEM

If possible, the ADR systems design team should include principled negotiation as one of the first processes to be used by disputants. The systems design team may recommend, for example, requiring disputants to negotiate before proceeding to other ADR processes. Obviously, not all disputants will be trained in principled negotiation. As a result, to familiarize employees with principled negotiation, the organization may have to invest in education and training in principled negotiation. Training is discussed in more detail in Chapter 13.

If the parties to the dispute are familiar with principled negotiation, they should be encouraged to attempt to defuse the conflict before it escalates, and before tensions become too high. Familiarizing employees of an organization with principled negotiation can therefore be a preventative measure, reducing the level of conflict that requires outside intervention.

If the disputants can resolve the dispute themselves, without the help of others, they will usually feel better about the process and as a result, they will be more likely to implement the result.

Case Study: Bank of Montreal

For the Bank of Montreal ADR system, both bank managers and Community Banking Managers attempt to negotiate a creative settlement with the small business customer as a first step in dispute resolution. If they do not settle the dispute, they can proceed to other processes. Many senior BOM officials have received training in principled negotiation.

Case Study:
Ontario Human Rights Commission

When a complaint is lodged with the Ontario Human Rights Commission, the complainant and respondent can attempt to negotiate a resolution to the dispute. If they are unsuccessful, the more formal dispute resolution process at the OHRC commences.

S U M M A R Y

INTEREST-BASED NEGOTIATION

- there are seven elements of principled negotiation:

  1. Alternatives (BATNA) — Disputants should determine what they will do if they do not reach agreement with the other disputant.
  2. Interests — Focus on interests rather than positions; ask "why" and "why not."
  3. Options — Brainstorm to generate as many creative options as possible.
  4. Legitimacy — Search for benchmarks, external standards, and objective criteria to help choose from among the options and ensure that disputants are being treated fairly.
  5. Communication — Avoid the word "but."
     - use paraphrasing where possible.
  6. Relationship — Be soft on the people, hard on the problem.
  7. Commitment — Commit only at the end of the negotiation, after reviewing all of the options.

- consider training potential disputants in principled negotiation
- consider requiring disputants to attempt to negotiate a resolution to their dispute before they use other dispute resolution processes

CHAPTER 8

Interest-Based Mediation

The process most commonly linked with ADR and ADR systems design is interest-based mediation. Mediation is facilitated negotiation. Interest-based mediation is principled negotiation with a negotiation expert, a mediator, who can assist the disputants to overcome any obstacles during their negotiation.

Mediation is not a binding process; the dispute will only be resolved if the disputants resolve it on mutually agreeable terms. For most mediations, the disputants can choose to leave the mediation at any time (though there is some "mandatory" mediation for litigation in some jurisdictions). If mediation does not yield a solution to the dispute, the disputants can resort to a binding process.

THE MEDIATION PROCESS

Although there are a number of models for interest-based mediation, they all attempt to determine the disputants' interests in the hope that the disputants and mediator will develop creative solutions that satisfy the interests. One model of mediation is a seven-stage model discussed below. The seven stages are:

1. Setting the Table;

2. Storytelling;

3. Determining Interests;

4. Determining the Issues;

5. Brainstorming Options;

6. Selecting an Option; and

7. Closure.

1. Setting the Table

In interest-based mediation, the mediator will set the table both literally and figuratively. In a literal sense, the mediator is responsible for the physical surroundings at the mediation, to ensure that the table is set (with pens, paper, coffee, and so on). If the disputants are comfortable, they will be more likely to participate effectively in the mediation process.

In a figurative sense, the mediator will also set the table by explaining the process to the disputants and trying to make them at ease with the mediator's approach.

In explaining the process, the mediator will likely outline the various stages involved in the process. The mediator will also explain that his or her role is as an impartial and neutral party. That is, he or she is not a judge and will not make a determination for the disputants. Rather, the mediator will simply facilitate the process, and the disputants will resolve the dispute. They will need to persuade each other, not the mediator, of the merits of their situations.

The mediator may also explore with the disputants whether they have the authority to resolve the problem themselves, or whether someone else in the organization needs to approve any settlement. If the latter is the case, disputants may agree that if they reach a tentative agreement at the end of the mediation, they will adjourn in order to obtain the necessary approvals, and reconvene later.

During this phase, the mediator will likely also set some ground rules for the disputants, such as only one person may speak at a time. Enforcing this seemingly simple ground rule may be the most important role that the mediator can play. Requiring disputants to listen to each other can allow for a fluid dialogue, an opportunity to understand each other's concerns, and a chance to develop unexplored options.

SPEAKING ONE AT A TIME

A colleague of mine once told me about a "negative" experience at a mediation. He was a lawyer in a personal injury claim and had attempted without success to settle the case by negotiating with the opposing lawyer. The two sides then decided to attempt mediation.

My colleague was frustrated that the mediator "did nothing" except enforce ground rules that required one person to speak at a time. I told him that it was unfortunate he had had a negative experience, and asked whether the case had gone to trial yet. He answered, "No, it settled at the mediation—but it had nothing to do with the mediator, I'm sure."

If parties are forced to listen to each other, that can sometimes be enough to allow them to reach a satisfactory resolution to their conflict.

A second ground rule that is often established in voluntary mediations is that disputants can leave the mediation at any time. This reassures disputants that they will not be coerced into a solution that they find unpalatable. The mediator may also suggest that the disputants refrain from personal attacks, though they should discuss concerns and feelings openly.

The mediator will likely also explain that some of the mediation will occur with everyone in the same room, while some of the mediation may take place in private meetings with the mediator, which are called "caucuses." Caucusing is discussed later in this chapter.

For most mediations, the mediator will explain that information discussed in the mediation is confidential, so that nothing can be disclosed outside the mediation that would not be discoverable by other means without prejudice. This means that disputants are not permitted to use the fact that a concession was made in a mediation to their advantage at a later arbitration or in litigation.

In addition, the mediator will tell the disputants that the mediator cannot be called as a witness at a future proceeding (such as an arbitration), and that the mediator's notes cannot be subpoenaed.

Some mediations, called "open mediations" are not confidential. In those mediations (usually involving marital disputes), information disclosed to the mediator or to the other party can be used in later proceedings.

By setting these ground rules, the mediator introduces the process to the disputants, puts them at ease, and attempts to gain their cooperation in listening to one another, being open to persuasion, and being creative.

2. Storytelling

Each disputant will then have an opportunity to express his or her perspective on the dispute. In many cases, disputants may not have had the opportunity to express to the other disputant how the conflict has affected them, and how they feel about the situation. The storytelling can be cathartic since it allows an opportunity to vent frustrations, express concerns, and release stress.

The storytelling can be relatively short (approximately 10 to 20 minutes) or it can take significantly longer, depending on the issues in the dispute and the level of emotion involved.

Anger, tears, frustration, and other extreme emotions may be expressed in the storytelling. The mediator will let the disputants talk, ensure that there are no interruptions, and may take notes about interests and preliminary ideas for settlement that arise during the storytelling.

THE STORY NEEDS TO BE TOLD

In one of my early mediations, I was asked to help resolve a dispute relating to the negligent construction of a house. The homeowner was suing the contractor, architect, and city inspector (for failing to notice the deficiencies on inspection). Because we were under tight time constraints, I asked the parties to tell their stories briefly, which they did.

After a couple of hours, we were very close to reaching a deal. The homeowner then said to the contractor, "You know, if only you had returned my phone calls, litigation would not have been necessary." The contractor then complained about the harassment he had received from the homeowner. I realized that before a final deal could be reached, the disputants needed to vent their frustrations. We resumed the storytelling, and the parties eventually resolved their differences.

This incident taught me the importance of allowing enough time for storytelling, even when there are tight time constraints.

3. Determining Interests

The mediator will then ask the disputants questions to clarify the perceptions and identify the underlying interests. Some mediators will list the disputants' interests on a flipchart or whiteboard for them to acknowledge and correct. Disputants will not always be forthcoming with their interests; they may attempt to hide their true concerns, advocating that their positions should be accepted. The mediator may meet with the disputants in private caucus to determine whether there are any hidden interests.

When attempting to uncover interests, mediators may use active listening techniques, as discussed in Chapter 7. Active listening will increase the disputants' comfort level since they will recognize that the mediator is listening to and understanding their concerns.

The mediator may then list the disputants' joint interests. Disputants usually focus on their differences, not their shared goals and interests. Joint interests may include resolving the conflict fairly, avoiding a long or expensive dispute resolution process, and preserving or enhancing reputations and relationships.

4. Determining the Issues

After the mediator has attempted to uncover the disputants' interests, the disputants will try to agree on the issues to be determined in the mediation. The mediator may suggest the issues, and ask the disputants whether they agree. The mediator will attempt to phrase issues as neutrally as possible, as joint problem-solving statements, and will try not to polarize disputants by phrasing issues so that they could be answered with a "yes" or "no." Phrases such as "how to deal with..." or "determining what to do about..." are common in issues. If possible, the mediator will frame the issues in terms of satisfying the disputants' interests. For example, the issue in a mediation between a supervisor and employee about mandatory overtime could be, "How to ensure that the company's work is complete and allow the employee to satisfy childcare obligations."

The issues may need to be revised as the mediation proceeds, and new issues may need to be added.

5. Brainstorming Options

Mediators will usually recommend brainstorming options that may satisfy the disputants' interests. The mediator will usually enforce the ground rules discussed in the previous chapter (no commitment to any option that is generated, and no criticism of options as they are being proposed), and encourage the disputants to be creative and even outrageous in their suggestions.

The mediator may or may not participate in generating options. Some mediators believe that since they are responsible for the process, not the substance of the mediation, they should not generate potential solutions. They fear that they may lose their neutrality if they generate options that are perceived to favour one side.

Other mediators believe, however, that the benefits outweigh any concerns. The mediator may have creative ideas that the disputants have not considered, and these ideas could assist the disputants to resolve their controversy. The disputants may be too deeply entrenched in their positions, or blinded by anger and frustration, to see viable options that a neutral third party may recognize.

6. Selecting an Option

Once the options are generated, the mediator will allow the disputants to assess the options and comment on options that may be feasible or impractical. During this stage of the mediation, the mediator may focus the disputants on objective criteria or benchmarks to assist them in selecting a viable option, and one that is perceived as fair by both disputants.

The mediator will not automatically eliminate an option when a disputant criticizes it. Instead, he or she will explore the reasons for the objection and invite them to suggest other options that satisfy their concerns.

The process of assessing options is not always straightforward or easy. Disputants may assess options in relation to their ideal solution or their originally stated position. The mediator may then discuss with disputants (often in private caucus) that the relevant decision for each disputant is not whether a particular option is ideal, but whether it is better than his or her BATNA.

7. Closure

If the disputants identify an option that is better than their respective BATNAs, they will likely commit to the option as a way to resolve the dispute.

If the disputants reach an agreement, the disputants can put their agreement in writing. The parties can then determine, with the assistance of the mediator, what steps they need to take to implement the agreement.

If there is no agreement, the mediator can assist the disputants to determine whether there are any issues that they can agree on. The mediator can then help the disputants determine their course of action to resolve outstanding issues.

Moving from Stage to Stage

Mediation does not usually involve a linear transition from one stage of the mediation to the next. Instead, the mediation may jump from storytelling, to options, to interests, and then back to storytelling. Each mediation develops its own flow, and the mediator will facilitate the process to allow an open exchange of concerns, ideas, and proposals.

WHAT'S THE RENT?

Returning to an example presented earlier, a land-lord and a tenant were disputing the appropriate amount of rent to be paid. The disputants claimed that their interests were in having a high (landlord) or low (tenant) rent. The tenant rejected the options proposed by the landlord, which the landlord claimed were based on comparable leases for similar properties. The tenant said that the options were unreasonable, since tenants in those properties were provided with timely snow removal and appropriate lighting (these being unsatisfied interests). Although the mediation was in the "Option" stage, it was clear that interests had not been fully explored. When the landlord learned of the interests, he agreed to accommodate them, and the parties resolved their dispute by agreeing to be bound by the opinion of a particular real estate agent with respect to market value of the rent.

Caucusing

There may be times during mediation when the mediator will want to meet separately with one of the disputants. The extent to which caucusing (private meetings between a disputant and the mediator) is used depends on the mediator and the progress that is being made when the disputants are together (in joint session). Some mediators prefer a model of mediation where the disputants go into caucus early in the process—soon after the storytelling or even earlier. In this model, the mediator may use the caucus to learn as much confidential information as possible from each of the parties to assist in brokering a settlement.

Extensive use of caucuses is sometimes referred to as "conciliation" or "shuttle diplomacy." This approach may be necessary where there is such a significant power imbalance that the integrity of the process would be jeopardized if the disputants remained in the same room throughout the mediation. For example, where one disputant alleges that the other is violent, it would usually be inappropriate to have both parties in one room.

Other mediators prefer a model in which the disputants stay in the same room throughout the mediation process. These mediators believe that by working out their differences together, the disputants can improve their relationship. Many mediators have adopted a model in which caucusing may occur when necessary, but joint sessions will be the norm. Generally, the amount of caucusing in a mediation depends on the circumstances; specifically, the level of antagonism, the ability of the disputants to resolve their differences together, the importance of any future relationship, and any potential power imbalance.

In order to encourage disputants to be candid in caucus, the mediator may choose to implement a ground rule guaranteeing the confidentiality of any private information conveyed to the mediator. The ground rules for confidential disclosures in caucuses should be clarified at the beginning of the mediation, and again at the beginning of the first caucus for each disputant.

THE ONE TEXT

A particular style of mediation that has been used with increasing frequency over the last number of years is known as the One Text. The process is described in *Getting to Yes* (1992). Mediators use this approach when a number of issues are in dispute, and disputants do not want to concede on any issue without knowing what they will receive in return on other issues. The One Text was used successfully in 1976 to mediate the dispute between Israel and Egypt that resulted in the Camp David Accord.

A mediator who uses the One Text first ascertains the disputants' concerns and interests, either in joint session or private caucus. The mediator then drafts a possible solution, based on the expressed interests. The draft is presented to the disputants, not as a solution for them to accept, but as a draft for them to criticize.

The mediator then considers the criticism and feedback from the disputants, and attempts to improve the draft. A revised draft is then be presented to the disputants for their feedback and criticism.

This process continues until the mediator believes that he or she can no longer improve the draft. At that time, the draft will be presented as a proposal for each disputant to accept or reject. At this stage, the disputants recognize that if they reject the draft, the mediation will be over. If they accept the draft, they accept the benefits and pay the costs as stipulated.

There are dangers to using the One Text. First, the disputants give significant control to the mediator who is drafting the agreement. The mediator may or may not understand the interests of the disputants, and yet is proposing appropriate trade-offs. Second, if a disputant rejects the final draft, the mediation is over.

On the positive side, the One Text can be an effective tool in overcoming hurdles to resolving complex, multi-issue and multi-party disputes.

SELECTING APPROPRIATE MEDIATORS

When ADR systems include a mediation process, the organization must select appropriate mediators. The issue of whether it is preferable to use mediators from within or outside the organization was discussed in Chapter 5.

Regardless of the source of the mediators, they should be trained in mediation, and be familiar with the organizational culture. They should also have sufficient understanding of the subject area of the disputes to communicate intelligently and effectively with the disputants. This is not to say that the mediator must have an intimate knowledge of the subject matter in dispute, since the mediator is the expert in process, not the expert in substance. Rather, the mediator's role is to facilitate the negotiation, not provide the solution.

If the organization decides to select an external mediator, there are a number of sources for referrals. Organizations such as the Arbitration and Mediation Institute of Canada, the American Arbitration Association, and the Canadian Foundation for Dispute Resolution provide lists of qualified neutrals. Alternatively, ADR firms can compile lists based on specified criteria. Fees for external mediators can range from zero (volunteer) to about $500/hour (for some respected retired judges). Generally, though, fees range from $100 to $300/hour or $1,500 to $3,500/day.

Sometimes organizations have an ombudsperson, who is a hybrid between an internal and an external mediator. Although he or she is an employee, the ombudsperson is often perceived as independent from the organization, and usually has the autonomy and ability to keep information confidential, even from senior people. To facilitate the resolution of a dispute, an ombudsperson may mediate, or may perform an independent investigation.

INTEGRATING MEDIATION INTO AN ADR SYSTEM

Many organizations can benefit from integrating mediation into their dispute resolution systems. Interest-based mediation should occur early in a dispute, before there has been a determination of rights. To establish a mediation process, an organization will need easily accessible mediators (either

on-site or by telephone), facilities to conduct the mediation (either on-site or off-site), and a co-ordinator to
schedule the mediations. For most disputes, mediations can
be scheduled for four to six hours. For complicated multi-
party disputes, a longer period, such as a full day, may be
needed.

The quality of mediation that is provided and the
sophistication of the system will depend on the organization's budget for the resolution of disputes.

Case Study: Bank of Montreal

The Bank of Montreal decided to offer mediation to
small business customers who were unable to
negotiate a satisfactory agreement with the bank manager or Community Banking Manager. The bank maintains a list of external (non-bank employee) mediators,
who are available to mediate across Canada. Stitt Feld
Handy Houston compiled the list based on the criteria
that the mediator should have mediation training and
experience, and be familiar with banking issues.

Mediations are scheduled for four to six hours, and
the bank manager or Community Banking Manager rep-
resents the bank at the mediations. A tentative resolution to the dispute reached at the mediation leads to
an adjournment to obtain the bank's formal approval.

Because BOM was concerned that a small business
customer may sell or encumber assets during the
mediation process, the bank required that: a) the small

business owners agree in writing to preserve any assets secured by the bank until the dispute resolution process concludes; b) the small business owners be entitled, however, to operate in the ordinary course of business: and c) the bank agree not to enforce its security during the process (unless there is evidence that the small business owner is acting fraudulently).

Case Study:
Ontario Human Rights Commission

The Ontario Human Rights Commission also implemented a mediation program to resolve discrimination complaints. The process can only be employed if all disputants agree to participate, and mediators are internal (OHRC employees), except where the OHRC is a party to the dispute. The mediation must occur within 90 days of the filing of the complaint, and if mediation does not result in an agreement among the parties, an OHRC investigator would be appointed.

S U M M A R Y

INTEREST-BASED MEDIATION

- facilitated negotiation with an expert trained in negotiation and mediation to act as a mediator
- process includes:

1. Setting the Table — explaining the process, the mediator's role, and establishing ground rules

2. Storytelling — opportunity for the disputants to present their perspectives and express emotions

3. Determining Interests — mediator will ask questions to attempt to determine the disputants' interests

4. Determining the Issues — issues to be framed in terms of satisfying the disputants' interests

5. Brainstorming Options — disputants (and sometimes mediators) will attempt to generate potential solutions to the conflict

6. Selecting an Option — disputants can use objective criteria to choose an option that satisfies their interests

7. Closure — the disputants should reduce their agreement to writing, or may need to plan future dispute resolution processes

- stages may not follow in a consecutive order
- caucusing (or private meetings) may occur with the mediator
- the One Text can be used when there are multiple issues or many parties
- the mediator should be sufficiently familiar with the substance of the dispute to communicate effectively with the disputants
- interest-based mediation should occur early in the dispute

CHAPTER 9

Rights

If interest-based processes do not resolve the conflict, disputants should turn to rights-based processes. In rights-based processes, a person other than the disputants determines who is correct or who should win; that is, a third party makes a judgment on the disputant's rights.

Rights-based processes can be either advisory (non-binding) or determinative (binding). Non-binding processes may be useful in providing disputants with a reality check or an unbiased assessment of the relative strengths of their positions. Binding processes provide finality as the disputants agree to be bound by and carry out the determination of a third party.

NON-BINDING PROCESSES

Some processes determine the rights of the disputants, but do not result in a binding decision. These processes should be incorporated into the ADR system after interest-based processes and before binding processes. Some of these processes are discussed below.

Rights-Based Mediation

An interest-based mediator facilitates the disputants' working together to settle their dispute. A rights-based mediator provides disputants with a non-binding opinion about how the mediator believes the dispute would be resolved if it were submitted to a binding rights-based process. The opinion may encourage the disputants to be less forceful about their positions, and to make concessions that will lead to a settlement.

In a rights-based mediation, disputants present facts to the mediator, arguing the merits of their cases. The mediator then provides his or her opinion to both (or all) of the disputants. Much of the mediation may then take place in caucus, where the mediator will attempt to persuade the disputants to alter their stances. The process is therefore sometimes referred to as "muscle mediation."

Rights-based mediators need a solid understanding of the substance of the dispute. Ideally, they are also expert in giving determinations based on conflicting information. As a result, rights-based mediators are often former judges, senior lawyers, or experienced business people.

Where disputants have unrealistic expectations, the rights-based mediation may cause the disputants to reassess.

In some situations, however, rights-based mediation can widen the gap between the disputants. For example, when a disputant hears a non-binding opinion in his or her favour, that person may become less willing to either compromise or consider other options. The other person, however, may not accept the opinion of the mediator, believing that the mediator did not fully understand the argument, and hoping that someone else will decide differently.

Early Neutral Evaluation

Early neutral evaluation (ENE) is similar to rights-based mediation. A respected neutral evaluates the likely outcome of the dispute if it were to proceed to a binding rights-based process. Unlike the rights-based mediator, the neutral in ENE leaves the disputants to attempt to negotiate a resolution to their dispute after providing an opinion. Although rights-based processes should generally be used after interest-based processes have failed, ENE can occur early in a dispute, before disputants have solidified their positions, and before their emotions have become too strong. Like rights-based mediation, ENE can be used as a reality check for disputants with unrealistic expectations.

Fact Finding

At times, a purely factual dispute requires someone to resolve incompatible versions of fact. A neutral fact finder can investigate, review documents, and interview witnesses to determine the facts. He or she can then present an oral or written report to the disputants, and to others in authority in the organization (if appropriate). The mere existence of the fact-finding process may act as an incentive for disputants to present their facts accurately, in order to avoid the potential stigma associated with a finding that the disputant had inaccurately reported facts.

Fact finders can be internal employees or external consultants. For example, the City of Toronto is an organization that employs external fact finders. City fact finders investigate internal harassment complaints. The external fact finder provides a written report so that the City can deal appropriately with the employee who is allegedly harassing another employee.

Mini-trials

The mini-trial is commonly used to resolve disputes between organizations, as opposed to disputes within organizations. There is a judicial mini-trial, in which a judge assists disputants to resolve disputes, and a private mini-trial, in which the court is not involved.

Judicial Mini-trials

In a judicial mini-trial, lawyers present abbreviated versions of their cases before a judge. The lawyers argue the law and tell the judge what they expect the witnesses will say. The judge then helps the disputants negotiate a solution to the dispute, based in part on his or her assessment of the legal arguments presented.

In Alberta, the judicial mini-trial has now become part of the court process. Judges are required, as part of their job, to preside over mini-trials in cases where the Chief Justice (or his or her delegate) determines that a mini-trial would be appropriate. Mini-trials have proven particularly successful in resolving disputes in personal injury litigation.

Private Mini-trials

In a private mini-trial, each disputing organization appoints a senior person from that organization who has not yet been involved in the dispute. These two individuals sit, sometimes in the presence of a respected third party (such as a retired judge or respected lawyer), and the three people hear the lawyers present brief summaries of their cases. After the presentations, the two senior people meet privately, with the respected neutral, and attempt to work out a solution to the conflict. Because the senior people have not been involved with the dispute, they may not have as strong emotions as their colleagues who were unable to resolve the conflict. The neutral can act as either an interest-based or a rights-based mediator, to help the organizations resolve their conflict.

Mini-trials are particularly effective and useful in resolving complex disputes between large organizations, where the organizations expect that there will be a future relationship. Although they have become popular in a number of U.S. states, such as New York, they have yet to gain widespread acceptance in Canada.

BINDING PROCESSES

If disputants cannot agree on a resolution to their conflict, through either interest-based or non-binding rights-
based approaches, a decision will need to be imposed on
them. In a binding rights-based process, a third party, usually impartial, is asked to make a decision that the disputants agree to honour. Binding rights-based processes
necessarily end the dispute. They should therefore always
occur as the final step in the dispute resolution system.

Courts and Tribunals

A default rights-based process involves litigation (going to
court) where the parties ask a judge to make a decision.
This process will be used if no other process is mandated by
the organization or agreed to by the disputants. Throughout the litigation process, certain procedural safeguards are
designed to ensure that the process is fair, regardless of the
outcome. Unfortunately, these safeguards can often result
in significant expense for disputants.

Administrative tribunals provide final, binding decisions, though the procedures are more flexible than the
civil litigation process.

A Superior Decides

A common and often appropriate binding process is having
a superior or another respected person in the organization
decide the outcome of the dispute.

The superior must have enough information to allow
him or her to make an informed decision. This information

can be provided to the superior either in person or in writing. The superior then decides how to resolve the dispute, and the disputants agree to abide by the decision.

Especially where disputes are common and relate to relatively insignificant issues (from the perspective of the senior people) in the organization, a decision by a superior can be efficient, inexpensive, and effective. A process that requires a superior to decide can also be used where the organization needs to maintain the ability to resolve disputes quickly and does not want to delegate that power to an external individual.

Arbitration

In an arbitration, a neutral arbitrator (or arbitrators) hears the arguments of the disputants, either directly from them or from their representatives (lawyers, union representatives, and so on), and then makes a decision. The disputants agree to be bound by the arbitrator's decision.

Arbitrations are governed in each province or state and internationally by legislation which mandates some of the rules for arbitration, and suggests other rules that will apply absent agreement of the disputants to the contrary. Arbitrations are similar to trials, but they may be less formal with fewer procedural safeguards, if the parties so agree.

Arbitrations can take many forms. The level of formality depends on the desire of the disputants, and the preferences of the arbitrator. If the disputants can agree on the rules for the arbitration, they can require the arbitrator to proceed as they have agreed (provided their agreement does not run contrary to legislation and there is procedural fairness). If the disputants agree to arbitrate but cannot agree on the rules for the arbitration, the arbitrator will decide (subject to requirements in the governing legislation).

There may be a single arbitrator, or each disputant may select one arbitrator and the two arbitrators will select the third arbitrator. However, it would be rare for organizations to set up a process with three arbitrators. For organizational disputes, it will usually be unnecessary to incur the expense and endure the structure of having three arbitrators.

A hallmark of arbitration is procedural fairness; in other words, the process used to achieve a result must be fair, regardless of the outcome. The arbitrator must ensure procedural fairness. If the process is not fair, one of the disputants could go to court and have the arbitration decision set aside.

The arbitrator hears evidence and makes determinations of fact (decides what has occurred if there is a dispute about the facts). If there is a dispute about the appropriate application of the law, the arbitrator must also resolve that dispute. Sometimes disputants have representatives argue for them; at other arbitrations, disputants represent themselves. Sometimes witnesses are asked questions; sometimes there are no witnesses and the disputants tell the arbitrator what the witnesses would say. The process can be as complex as necessary.

The duration of an arbitration depends on the rules for the arbitration and the complexity of the issues in dispute. Some arbitrations are completed in less than a day while others take several months.

If the systems design team integrates arbitration into its ADR system, it will need to establish the rules for the arbitration. The rules could be established before the ADR system is implemented by the systems design team so that the arbitration can be quick and efficient. For example, the design team could recommend that the organization require that arbitrations last no more than six hours, that each disputant call only one witness, and that all evidence be admissible. Or, the design team could allow the disputants to establish their own process rules for the arbitrator.

The design team will also need to determine how the arbitrator will be selected, and whether the arbitrator will be selected from within or outside the organization. Regardless of the source, the arbitrator should have substantive knowledge of the issues in dispute. He or she will need to determine who is right and who is wrong, and should have as much expertise as possible about the type of controversy being arbitrated. The arbitrator must also be neutral. He or she must be someone who does not have a vested interest in the outcome of the dispute, nor a vested interest in one of the disputants succeeding or failing within the organization.

PROCESSES THAT COMBINE INTEREST-BASED AND RIGHTS-BASED APPROACHES

Where disputants want the benefits of an interest-based process and the finality of a binding rights-based process, they may attempt a process that facilitates the exploration of interests and, if the disputants cannot consensually resolve the dispute, provides a binding resolution.

Mediation/Arbitration (Med/Arb)

In Med/Arb, an interest-based mediator first attempts to help the disputants negotiate a resolution to the dispute. If the mediation does not resolve all outstanding issues, the mediator then transforms himself or herself into an arbitrator with the power to make a binding decision. From the outset, the disputants know that this process will produce a final decision, regardless of whether there is agreement at the mediation.

Usually, in Med/Arb, the same person who mediated becomes the arbitrator. There may, therefore, be disadvantages to Med/Arb. For example, because the mediator may be forced to become a decision-maker if the mediation is unsuccessful, the disputants may be reluctant to confide in the mediator about potential weaknesses in their cases. The mediator also may not receive honest input from the disputants about their assessment of the strengths and weaknesses of their cases. In addition, the disputants may be more focused on persuading the mediator/arbitrator than in negotiating with each other.

Further, the disputants may focus too closely on the words used by the mediator, in an attempt to infer a likely result if arbitration becomes necessary. This focus may hinder settlement possibilities. At the same time, the mediator must be careful not to make comments that could indicate a bias or to otherwise suggest that the decision in a potential arbitration has already been made.

On the other hand, the arbitrator will not have to spend time learning the facts, if the issues proceed to arbitration, since he or she would already be familiar with them through the mediation process. This may result in cost savings for the disputants.

Case Study: Bank of Montreal

The Bank of Montreal needed to be able to make a determination about credit if negotiation and interest-based mediation were unsuccessful in resolving the dispute between the small business customer and the bank. The bank could not afford to give a third party the power to decide whether and how the bank's money should be loaned. As a result, the bank manager and the Community Banking Manager retained the authority to make a final determination about withdrawing or reducing credit.

Case Study: Ontario Human Rights Commission

The OHRC mediations needed to involve a combination of interest-based and rights-based processes. While the mediator would explore interests and needs behind positions, the mediator could also provide information about a likely outcome at a Commission hearing, and information about results of other hearings where similar issues were addressed.

If the dispute between a complainant and an alleged discriminating respondent were not resolved at mediation, a different member of the OHRC, an investigator, would attempt to determine the facts that had led to the complaint. After the investigator performed fact finding, the investigator would attempt to persuade the complainant and respondent to proceed with courses of action that the investigator believed would be appropriate (based on that investigator's experiences).

If no resolution were achieved, legislation provided that a binding rights-based process, a hearing before the Commission, would be conducted.

S U M M A R Y

RIGHTS

• if interest-based processes fail to yield a solution, disputants can have a neutral party determine rights

NON-BINDING PROCESSES

• rights-based mediation — a neutral assesses the case and attempts to persuade disputants to make concessions
• early neutral evaluation — a neutral provides an early opinion about the outcome of a dispute
• fact finding — a neutral person investigates disputed facts and makes a report
• mini-trials — a judge or other neutral hears summaries of cases and assists disputants to resolve the conflict

BINDING PROCESSES

• a superior decides — can be used for less significant disputes and where the organization needs to maintain the ability to resolve the dispute
• arbitration — a neutral person hears evidence, makes determinations of fact and law, and produces a binding judgment

RIGHTS-BASED AND INTEREST-BASED

• Med/Arb — if mediation does not result in agreement, the mediator becomes an arbitrator and makes a binding decision

CHAPTER 10

Exits and Re-entries

Interest-based processes do not always resolve a conflict. These processes should not be permanently discarded, however, when they fail to produce a resolution; there should be set times later in the dispute resolution system when the disputants "loopback" to one or more of the previously unsuccessful interest-based processes before a final rights-based determination is made.

Regardless of the processes designed to resolve the conflict, the system should contain mechanisms so that disputants can exit a rights-based process and re-enter an interest-based process that had been used earlier, and had failed. This is a "loopback." In addition, the system should provide time for sober reflection, or "cooldown" periods.

LOOPBACKS

If interest-based processes such as negotiation and mediation fail, the disputants will need a binding rights-based
process to decide the dispute. There may be opportunities during the rights-based process to loop back to an
interest-based process before a resolution has been
imposed on the disputants.

For example, a system can be designed with an arbitration process that loops back to interest-based negotiation. The arbitrator could hear the arguments from the
disputants, and then write two sets of reasons, each leading to a decision in favour of a different disputant. The
arbitrator could inform the disputants that one of these
sets of reasons leads to the *real* decision, and that the other
leads to the opposite decision (the one that the arbitrator
did not reach). The arbitrator could place the real decision in a sealed envelope and hold the envelope for 48
hours, giving the disputants a final opportunity to resolve
their dispute consensually using negotiation.

In this case, the disputants would have heard reasons and
a decision in their favour, and reasons and a decision against
them. During the 48 hours, they could discuss whether there
was an interest-based solution that better met their needs
than gambling on which decision was in the envelope. If the
disputants do not agree on a resolution within 48 hours, the
arbitrator would reveal the actual decision.

The dispute resolution system could also provide for a
loopback to interest-based mediation before a rights-based
decision is rendered. For example, an arbitrator could suspend the arbitration while a mediator assists the disputants

to attempt to resolve their dispute, even if the disputants had previously attempted mediation and had not reached consensus.

Loopbacks in a system should not be so onerous and bureaucratic that their benefits are outweighed by the harm that results from an elongated system. Instead, they should be designed to operate within the time constraints inherent in the system.

COOLDOWNS

When attempts to resolve conflict have failed, disputants need time to reflect on the consequences. They will need time to consider their options and make informed decisions about how to proceed. ADR systems should therefore allow for cooldowns or cooling-off periods during which disputants can reflect and analyze. Cooldown periods can vary in length, depending on the urgency of resolving the conflict. During this period, disputants can take time to think about their BATNAs, whether to continue with the dispute, how to proceed, and whether the potential consequences of moving to the next process justify the necessary time and expense.

They may voluntarily meet and discuss options for resolving their dispute. Even if the system does not create a formal process for consultation, the disputants may decide to reconsider previously discussed options, or develop new options.

Cooldown periods cannot be so long, however, that they prolong a dispute that should be resolved quickly. The

periods for cooldown must be reasonable in the circumstances. Cooldown periods may not be desirable at all, for
example, where assets are depleting.

Case Study: Bank of Montreal

In the Bank of Montreal credit dispute resolution
process, if the disputants could not negotiate a resolution to the dispute, there would be a cooldown period
between the end of negotiations and the start of a mediation. If negotiations were to break down, the business
customer would be given a list of qualified mediators,
and would be required to select a mediator within three
days of receiving the list. The mediation would take place
10 days after the mediator was selected. At any point
prior to the mediation, the disputants could re-enter
negotiations to attempt to resolve the dispute directly,
without the mediator's assistance.

If negotiation and mediation failed to achieve a
settlement of the credit dispute, there would be a
loopback to negotiation before the bank could reduce
or withdraw credit. The small business customer could
go to the office of the Vice Chairman in order to try
to negotiate a resolution of the dispute. If no satisfactory resolution were achieved there, the business customer could go to the Office of the Superintendent of
Financial Institutions.

Case Study:
Ontario Human Rights Commission

If a mediation at the Ontario Human Rights Commission did not result in a settlement, there would be a cooldown for a number of months to allow for a thorough investigation prior to a Commission hearing. The design team suggested that the OHRC consider allowing a loopback to mediation during the investigation, if the disputants and investigator thought such a loopback would be beneficial.

S U M M A R Y

EXITS AND RE-ENTRIES

- in the midst of a rights-based process, disputants may be required to loop back to an interest-based process
- loopbacks should operate within the time constraints of the system
- cooldowns should allow time for reflection and for considering BATNAs and previously rejected options

CHAPTER 11

Creativity

To develop a conflict management system, an organization must examine new ways of handling conflict—and this requires creativity. Finding creative ways to handle conflict can be difficult as many organizational structures do not promote creativity and because often there are rules in place. Rules can be helpful in creating parameters beyond which people should not operate, and they can provide an excuse when things do not work out. However, rules can also inhibit creativity and stifle independent thought.

For better or for worse, the first rule of systems design is that there are no rules. In specific circumstances, the systems design team can and should disregard any of the suggestions in this book. The DIRECT approach provides guidelines, not to be followed blindly, but to be considered and adopted if they make more sense than others.

Designing a conflict management system will give members of the design team opportunities to use creativity, explore, experiment, and consider innovative options. The types of processes, the rules in the processes, the people involved, and the cost structure are all opportunities for the design team to brainstorm and be creative. The design team should view obstacles in the systems design process as opportunities to find innovative and creative solutions.

There should be no limits on creativity. If an idea makes sense, it can be implemented even if it breaks a rule for an ADR process or for ADR systems design. That does not mean, of course, that all creative new ideas will work. Some will be successful while others will fail to achieve the organizational goals.

Case Study: Bank of Montreal

The Bank of Montreal systems design team was confronted with a number of difficult issues requiring creative solutions.

(a) Requirement to Stay at the Mediation

Mediation specialists sometimes suggest that a fundamental tenet of interest-based mediation is that the disputants be able to leave the mediation at any time if they feel that they are not comfortable with the process, if they feel that they are being bullied, or if they simply want to proceed with the next stage of the dispute resolution process. This safeguard provides disputants with comfort and encourages them to participate in mediation.

For the BOM, however, it did not make sense to have a mediation process for the small business where the bank representative could come into the mediation, listen for a short time, and leave. If the process were to have appeal to the small business customer, the bank manager would have to be required to stay in the mediation for a set period.

The bank therefore decided, on the recommendation of the design team, to require its representative to remain in the mediation for at least the first four hours of mediation, even if during the entire process, the customer were using the mediation as an opportunity to complain. (In fact, venting is often necessary to allow disputants to release strongly held feelings and to allow them to think creatively.) The small business person was therefore assured that the bank representative would have to listen to the business person's concerns and proposals.

The design team believed that four hours was a reasonable time for the customer to make a case to the bank.

While the bank representative could not leave the mediation for four hours, the small business person could terminate the mediation at any time.

(b) Payment

Traditionally, there are two methods of paying the mediator's fee: each disputant pays half of the cost of the mediation, or one party pays the entire cost. Each option had potential advantages and disadvantages for the BOM. If each disputant were to pay half of the cost of the mediation, each disputant would have ownership of the mediation process and would feel that the mediator was somewhat responsible to them. If the small business person did not pay for the mediator, there may be at least an appearance that the mediator was a bank person, not responsible to the business person. In addition, since both the bank and the small business person were benefitting from the mediation, it was logical to have each party pay half of the cost.

On the other hand, small businesses were only being offered mediation in cases where they were having difficulty repaying their loans, and the cost of the mediation would pose more of a burden to them than it would to the bank. The bank did not want to make the mediation unaffordable for the small business.

As a result, the design team developed a payment scheme where the bank neither pays the entire cost of the mediation, nor does it split the cost with the small business customer. Instead, the bank pays for the initial three hours of the mediation, with the cost of the mediator's preparation time and any additional time being divided evenly between the bank and the small business.

In this way, the cost of the mediator would not be significant for the small business person (unless the mediation took a long period of time, which could only occur if the small business person wanted to continue the process beyond three hours), and the business person would have some ownership in the process.

(c) Choice of Mediator

People in the ADR community stress the importance of training and experience for mediators. Many suggest that a good mediator must have both training in mediation and experience. This is generally true. In the case of a mediator for BOM, the mediator also needed to have an understanding of banking and credit issues. As a result, the bank compiled a list of qualified neutrals who it believed could effectively mediate disputes between the bank and small business customers. People on the list were required to have training or experience mediating, and a familiarity with banking issues.

The design team was concerned, however, that in the midst of a dispute, the small business customer may not want to use a mediator who was approved by the bank because of a perception that the mediator may want to rely on the bank for future mediation work. The bank therefore decided, on the recommendation of the design team, that the small business person be able to select the mediator, either from the bank's pre-approved list, or from elsewhere. However, the mediator could not be a relative or employee of the small business person and would preferably have some mediation training or experience.

The design team knew that others in the mediation community would have concerns about the mediator selection process. Concerns would stem from the fear that untrained mediators would give mediation a bad name, or that the mediator could be biased against the bank (since there was no requirement for the mediator to be from a "neutral" pool of mediators). The design team's response to these concerns was as follows:

First, the mediator would often be selected from the bank's pre-approved list.

Second, in those situations where the business customers did not want to select anyone from the list, the reason was likely either a) the business people were so suspicious of the bank that they did not trust anyone on the bank's list; or b) the business people had had good experiences with other mediators, and wanted to retain them again. In either case, if the business people were required to choose someone from the bank's list, they would likely be uncomfortable with the mediator, be reluctant to disclose information, and not trust comments from the mediator. If the mediator were chosen by the business people, however, they would be more comfortable and would feel free to disclose confidential information to him or her. This mediator would therefore be more likely to be able to help the disputants find a solution. In addition, if the mediator conveyed information to the business people that they did not want to hear, the business people would be more likely to accept the information (and advice) from a mediator they had selected, than from a mediator from the bank's pre-approved list. Ultimately, the bank wanted the business people to be comfortable with the mediator and the mediation.

Third, the bank was under no obligation to accept any deal proposed at a mediation unless the bank determined that it was in its best interest to do so. It would therefore not be forced to accept a bad deal from a bad mediator. A deal could only be concluded in a mediation if the disputants agreed to the solution, and no solution could be imposed.

Fourth, the BOM's pre-approved list of mediators was not exhaustive. A mediator selected by business people could be as qualified as anyone on the list.

Case Study:
Ontario Human Rights Commission

The most significant challenge faced by the ADR systems design team for the Ontario Human Rights Commission related to the role of the mediator. By legislation, all OHRC staff (including a staff mediator) were required to protect the public interest, and could not support a resolution that was contrary to the public interest. The OHRC mediator, however, needed to be neutral and not take a position on issues. The OHRC budget did not allow for a second OHRC person to attend the mediation to represent the OHRC, and it did not allow for external mediators. As a result of its consultations, the design team learned that stakeholders wanted the mediator to be neutral, and they wanted the mediator to be able to keep confidential any information learned at the mediation.

On the recommendation of the design team, the OHRC decided that first, the mediator would be an interest-based mediator but would be permitted to provide information about the potential outcome at an OHRC hearing and information about outcomes of previous hearings.

Second, there was an "approval process" to ensure that the public interest would be protected. If a complaint, on its face, indicated that a public interest remedy might be required (where, for example, a complaint alleged that a theater did not allow for handicapped access, thus requiring a remedy so that all handicapped members of the public could gain access to the theater), any resolution at mediation would have to be approved by Commissioners (who were not involved in the mediation). Also, if there were an element of the resolution that required future action by the respondent (for example, taking courses, building ramps, changing policies), this resolution would require approval by Commissioners.

The Commissioners could ensure that the public interest were protected, and the mediators could remain neutral, and not disclose any confidential information.

Where the complaint, on its face, did not require a public interest remedy, and where the resolution did not require any future action by the respondent, a resolution could be approved by a manager (less senior than a Commissioner) who would approve the resolution if it satisfied the public interest.

SUMMARY

CREATIVITY

- in ADR systems design, there are no rules that cannot be broken in appropriate circumstances
- the design team can use such techniques as brainstorming to develop creative solutions

CHAPTER 12

Training and Evaluation

In order to use the ADR system productively, disputants, dispute resolvers, and other stakeholders need to understand the system itself and its processes. In almost all cases this will involve some education and training.

EDUCATION

Stakeholders both within and outside the organization will need information about the ADR system and its processes. People who will participate in the system need to know the parameters of the system and the rules within which they must operate. Their education should begin while the system is being designed, and they should be encouraged to provide input and suggestions.

Once the system has been designed, but before it has been implemented, the design team should meet again with internal and external stakeholders to discuss the proposed system and inform them of how their input affected the design of the system. The design team can explain that the design process is fluid, and that the system will be periodically revised to improve its effectiveness. The design team could then encourage stakeholders to participate in the new processes. Also, the organization could monitor the use of new processes compared with old processes, and publicly acknowledge employees who use the new processes.

The organization may also create penalties for those who resist the new system. In some circumstances, it may be necessary to make it clear that if there is recrimination against employees who use the new system, those responsible will be reprimanded. Any opponents to the new system, however, could be invited to present their concerns to the design team either orally or in writing.

Stakeholders should also be advised whom they can contact if they have difficulty accessing the new ADR system. Some members of the design team should be available for consultations to facilitate a smooth implementation of the system.

The design team can also inform stakeholders of any skills training opportunities that may be available so that the stakeholders can become comfortable with the new processes. The design team should also describe the processes that are to be used, when they can be used, and how they can be accessed. The design team can also present the benefits of the new processes, and descriptions of some successes that other organizations have achieved using the processes.

The systems design team may also provide written material for those who prefer to learn about the ADR system in more detail at their convenience.

Skills Training

Stakeholders who are likely to make significant use of the ADR system, either as neutrals or as participants, will need to be trained so that they can use the system effectively. Training can provide people with the necessary negotiation and mediation skills to use the new processes. Training may be conducted by companies that specialize in ADR training, or for larger companies, by the organization's own internal training team.

If necessary, training courses can be customized to meet each organizations's specific needs. Customized courses typically cost about $3,000 to $8,000 per day for up to twenty-four people.

If an organization is training fewer than 20 individuals, or if it cannot afford to have more than 20 people away from the organization at one time, it could send employees to attend public ADR courses that specialize in the necessary skills. Four-day courses in negotiation or mediation range from $1,000 to $2,000 per person.

Interest-Based Negotiation Training

Since many ADR processes are based on negotiation, the training process should begin by providing participants with a solid grounding in interest-based negotiation. Even though people negotiate every day, they must think carefully about how they negotiate, and analyze the process of negotiation to identify how to improve their skills. A practical skill-based course in negotiation can improve the skills of both novice and skilled negotiators. To be effective, a course in negotiation should be at least three to five days in length.

Role-play exercises can contain generic scenarios with which participants are not familiar; the training need not focus only on the specific activities of the organization. Rather, the crucial element of the training is that it teach the generic skills necessary for participants to function effectively within the dispute resolution system. At the end of the training, participants can then discuss how the skills learned will apply to issues that the organization faces. The discussion can provide a summary and some context for the skills that participants have learned.

Although some people have an aversion to role playing, it can be effective in assisting participants to improve their interest-based negotiation skills.

Other Training

The organization should provide more advanced training (after negotiation training) to people who will act as neutrals in the dispute resolution system. Mediators will need to learn how to deal with difficult issues in mediation such as dealing with difficult or emotional disputants, addressing power imbalances, and maintaining neutrality in the face of strong feelings. They will also need to study practical skills such as setting ground rules and knowing when to caucus. Ideally, a mediation course should take at least three to five days (assuming participants have completed a negotiation course).

Arbitrators will have to learn how to conduct the arbitration process, hold a hearing, and ensure procedural fairness. They must also become familiar with the arbitration legislation in force in their province or state.

EVALUATION

An organization with a new ADR system will need to evaluate it to determine whether it is working effectively and whether it should be changed.

Go Back to Stakeholders

If time permits, the systems design team should consult stakeholders after the system has been designed but before it has been implemented to obtain stakeholders' views of the proposed system. Stakeholders may point out potential pitfalls in the proposal system that the design team had not considered.

The design team should assimilate the information, meet to discuss it, and tweak the system as necessary.

Commencing with a Pilot Project

To test the effectiveness of the system, the organization should initiate the system with a pilot project. After the pilot has been assessed, the organization will be better able to determine what the ADR system should look like, which new processes work effectively, and what changes must be made to address shortcomings.

Ideally, the pilot project should be conducted in an environment where there are a variety of disputes, some of which are intense. The designers should allow enough time for the pilot project so that they can conduct a valid assessment, and so the results will be perceived as accurate. ADR pilot projects last for one or two years, or can be shorter if required. If the pilot project will last more than a year, the assessors may be able to provide interim reports that can allow the organization to do an interim analysis before the assessment is complete. If it is not possible to have a pilot project involving a limited number of disputes (where, for example, the needs of the organization dictate radical and fast change), the design team should set a period of time as the pilot, and assess the system after the time has expired and the new processes have been used.

The Assessment

The purpose of the assessment is to determine whether the design team has met the organizational goals that were identified during the diagnosis.

The pilot project will only be as useful as the assessment of it. As with so many aspects of systems design, the assessment can be done internally or by consultants. Academics often have the time, expertise, and inclination to assist with assessments, and graduate students will sometimes volunteer their time to assist with or even conduct an assessment.

Ideally, the assessment should compare disputes that have proceeded through the new processes with a control group that has used the old processes. The assessment should explore whether cost savings and time reductions have resulted from the new system (quantitative analysis), and whether disputant satisfaction has increased (qualitative analysis).

It is important to plan the assessment at the beginning of the implementation of the system, not at the conclusion of the pilot project. The assessors need time to produce material and determine a timetable for their analysis.

The design team may want to include those who resist the new ADR processes in the assessment team. These individuals can focus the assessors on areas for improvement, and may become supporters of changes to the system if they feel they have had input into the changes that are made.

Tools For Assessment

Assessors use a number of tools to assess an ADR system. They may first accumulate objective quantitative data such as how many and how quickly disputes have been resolved.

Obtaining qualitative subjective data, however, can be more difficult. Where time and resources permit, the design team may conduct personal interviews of those who participated in the system. Disputants may also be asked to complete questionnaires about their experiences with the system. In either case, data should be obtained as soon as possible after the disputants have participated in the new ADR processes. The questions asked in questionnaires or personal interviews should relate to the beliefs and values of the organization in order to determine whether the system has met organizational objectives.

A sample questionnaire (used for an evaluation of a mediation pilot project in the Peel Small Claims Court) is provided at the end of this chapter.

The design team may also be able to observe some of the ADR processes and obtain important data that could assist with the analysis of the system.

Assessment of Mandatory Mediation In Ontario

In 1997, the Ontario Attorney-General announced mandatory mediation for all civil non-family actions in Ontario as a result of the findings of an assessment done of an ADR Pilot Project in Toronto. The two-year pilot project provided that cases would be randomly selected for court-annexed mediation, and Dr. Julie Macfarlane performed an assessment of the settlement rates and user satisfaction with mediation. She concluded that about twice as many mediated cases settled as did cases in the control group. She also found that mediated cases were resolved in approximately half the time of the cases in the control group.

Case Study: Bank of Montreal

The Bank of Montreal informed its employees of its new mediation process by sending written material to the bank's senior employees who deal with small business customers. The BOM also publicized its new process at the bank's branches.

A number of senior bank officials received interest-based negotiation training from training organizations across Canada. Since the bank was using only external mediators, no specialized mediation training for mediators was required.

The introduction of the mediation program for credit disputes was a form of a pilot project for the bank. The design team recommended an assessment of the program at a later date to determine whether the bank should expand the use of mediation to other areas in which disputes arise.

Case Study: Ontario Human Rights Commission

The Ontario Human Rights Commission introduced the ADR system to its employees at a joint meeting with the design team. The design team discussed its deliberations and conclusions, and addressed employees' concerns and questions.

Both investigators and mediators at the OHRC received negotiation training. In addition, OHRC mediators received advanced and context-specific mediation training.

The new system needed to be implemented throughout the province to attempt to improve the dispute resolution process immediately, and to dispose of some of the caseload. The OHRC retained a graduate student to assess the program after a six-month period. The student could work with the OHRC to prepare appropriate questionnaires and focus on areas where the OHRC anticipated stress on the system.

S U M M A R Y

TRAINING AND EVALUATION

- educate stakeholders about the system
  - hold a meeting
  - provide written material

- provide incentives to use the new system

- present success stories from other organizations

- provide interest-based negotiation training to people who participate repeatedly in interest-based processes

- mediators and arbitrators take more advanced training

- establish a pilot project to test system

- assessors should compare pilot project to control group

- assessors can look for cost savings, time reduction, and increase in user satisfaction

REGION OF PEEL
SMALL CLAIMS COURT
MEDIATION PILOT PROJECT

SURVEY

PART I

PRE-MEDIATION EXPERIENCE

1. Were you the **plaintiff** or the **defendant**?

   _____

2. Was this the **first time** you had been to a mediation?

              Yes   ❏   No   ❏

   If **no**, please describe the other time(s) you have attended at a mediation (What was the dispute about? Were you satisfied with the mediation process?):

   _____

   _____

   _____

   _____

3. Have you been involved as a plaintiff or defendant in other legal cases before?

              Yes   ❏   No   ❏

   If **yes**, how many other cases?

4. Have you been to court before?

              Yes   ❏   No   ❏

5. How would you describe that experience?

_____

_____

6. Did you feel you had enough information about how the mediation would work before the day of your mediation?

Yes ❏   No ❏

If **no**, what else would you want to have known?

_____

7. Was the written information you received before the mediation

understandable?   Yes ❏   No ❏
helpful?   Yes ❏   No ❏

If **no**, what was missing?_____

_____

8. Did you understand all of the terms in the Agreement to Mediate document that you signed before the mediation?   Yes ❏   No ❏

If **no**, please tell us what was not clear._____

_____

_____

9. Why did you choose to try mediation in your case? Please check as many boxes as are applicable.

It could save me time.   ❏
It could save me money.   ❏
It could lead to a better settlement.   ❏
I wanted to avoid a trial.   ❏
I thought I could do better at mediation.   ❏

I thought the other side would better understand
my case.   ❑

I thought I could be more active in a mediation
than a trial.   ❑

I was afraid of losing at a trial.   ❑

I wanted to be reasonable.   ❑

I wanted to achieve a more creative solution.   ❑

It would be less formal than court.   ❑

I was simply curious.   ❑

PART II

THE MEDIATION SESSION

10. Did you know your mediator was not a lawyer?

        Yes ❑   No ❑

11. Did it matter to you?

        Yes ❑   No ❑

12. Do you think if your mediator was trained as a lawyer
it would have been ...

more helpful   ❑

less helpful   ❑

no difference   ❑

13. A "coach" was present during some or all of your
mediation.

The coach was very active in the session.

        Yes ❑   No ❑

I don't remember the coach.

        Yes ❑   No ❑

Did you think your mediator needed a coach?

          Yes ❏   No ❏

Was it disruptive to have a coach present?

          Yes ❏   No ❏

Was he or she helpful?

          Yes ❏   No ❏

14. During the session, the mediator ...
(check as many as applicable)

put too much pressure on me to settle   ❏

was helpful in giving us ideas for settlement   ❏

was always neutral and showed no bias   ❏

asked good questions   ❏

helped me to understand the other person's
perspective   ❏

always understood what was happening   ❏

made the situation worse   ❏

was of no use   ❏

seemed to be on my side   ❏

seemed to be on the other person's side   ❏

15. During the mediation I ...

	Yes	No
was treated with respect by the mediator	❏	❏
had the chance to explain my situation	❏	❏
listened to the other side	❏	❏
met with the mediator alone	❏	❏
asked the coach for assistance	❏	❏

16. At the end of the mediation, when you met with the
Judge ...

	Yes	No
was he/she helpful in deciding if you should settle	❏	❏

did he/she make you feel pressured to settle ❑ ❑

did he/she answer any questions you had ❑ ❑

did he/she have some good ideas about the
terms of settlement ❑ ❑

did he/she explain what could happen if
the case went to trial ❑ ❑

did he/she make you feel you were doing
the right thing ❑ ❑

PART III

RESOLUTION

17. Did you reach a settlement?

                      Yes ❑   No ❑

If **yes, please continue**, if no, please go to question **20**.

18. Are you <u>still</u> satisfied with the settlement?

                      Yes ❑   No ❑

19. Do you think you would have done as well at trial?

                      Yes ❑   No ❑

20. If you did <u>not</u> reach a settlement, did the mediation ...

help narrow issues? Yes ❑   No ❑

give you a chance to rethink your case?

                      Yes ❑   No ❑

make the situation worse?

                      Yes ❑   No ❑

21. Did you settle after the mediation but before trial?

                      Yes ❑   No ❑

22. What happened at trial?_____

_____

_____

23. Would you go to another mediation?

Yes ❏   No ❏

24. Would you recommend mediation to others?

Yes ❏   No ❏

25. Would you be willing to pay for a mediation? (for a three-hour session)

Up to $25   ❏
Up to $50   ❏
Up to $100   ❏
Over $100   ❏
I would not be willing to pay for it.   ❏

26. Is there anything else you want to tell us? Please use this space to do so.

_____

_____

_____

_____

_____

_____

THANK YOU!

CHAPTER 13

ADR in External Disputes

Much of the material presented in this book relates to disputes that occur within organizations, among employees, or disputes for which the organization offers internal processes for resolution. This chapter, however, will examine how to deal with disputes between organizations—external disputes.

Organizations do not necessarily have control over external disputes. For disputes among members of an organization, the organization can set ground rules and require that employees abide by its rules. Where an organization has existing internal processes in place for resolution, disputants can become familiar with and even comfortable with the processes and the rules that govern them. For external disputes, however, it is not always possible to anticipate who the other disputant will be, what the issues will be, and what process will be most effective to deal with the dispute.

SETTING UP A SYSTEM BEFORE THE DISPUTE ARISES

Once a dispute arises, the parties involved often distrust each other and may be unable to agree which dispute resolution process to use. For example, when a process is proposed by one of the disputing parties, the other may reject it solely because the opponent suggested it. However, if organizations can agree, before a dispute arises, as to how they will resolve disputes that may arise, they can avoid time-consuming and expensive battles about process. When organizations are operating on good terms (and are having or expecting a profitable relationship), they are in the best position to design a process to deal with potential disputes.

When organizations enter into contracts, they can incorporate an ADR clause that stipulates the processes that will be used to resolve any disputes that arise. If there is no ADR clause in the contract, however, the disputants' recourse will often be civil litigation, even though it may not be in their best interests.

MULTI-STEP ADR CLAUSE

In order to craft an appropriate ADR clause for a contract, an organization should think about what it hopes to achieve with the clause. The organization may learn that it strives for processes that preserve rather than destroy the relationship (to allow the organizations to continue to deal with each other); that are relatively quick and inexpensive; that lead to a resolution that the organization is satisfied with; and that provide certainty about the result. Although no single process can accomplish all of these goals, a multi-step ADR clause can.

A multi-step clause provides an orderly use of different ADR processes. If the organizations do not resolve the dispute using the first process, they move to the next process, and continue to do so until the dispute is resolved. Multi-step ADR clauses usually begin with interest-based processes and conclude with a determinative rights-based process, with cooldown periods and loopbacks in between.

Negotiation

A logical first process in a multi-step ADR clause dealing with inter-organizational disputes requires the disputing parties to negotiate with each other. Negotiators (with authority to settle) should be given a reasonable amount of time, after they have learned the issues in dispute, to attempt to resolve the conflict to the satisfaction of both organizations. Ideally, the negotiators should be trained in interest-based negotiation. If the negotiators cannot resolve the dispute, they may enlist the services of a mediator to facilitate the negotiation.

Mediation

The ADR clause can also provide a time frame and guidelines for mediation. The clause may name a particular mediator (and an alternate in case the named mediator is unable or unwilling to act). The named mediator should have a style that is consistent with the disputants' approach. It will therefore be necessary to contact potential mediators to determine whether they practise interest-based or rights-based mediation, and whether they would be willing to act. If the organizations do not choose to select a mediator in advance, the ADR clause can require that a neutral dispute resolution organization provide a list of available mediators to the disputing parties, and that the parties independently rank the mediators and exchange lists. The mediator with the highest total ranking would be selected.

The clause can provide time limits for the selection of the mediator and the conduct of the mediation itself so that the process will occur within a reasonable time.

Other Non-binding Processes

Instead of mediation, an organization may prefer other non-binding processes such as the mini-trial, or early neutral evaluation to determine rights, but not to finally determine issues between the parties. The non-binding rights-based process may assist the disputants to become realistic about their approach to the dispute.

If the non-binding processes do not lead to a final settlement, the organizations will need to conclude the dispute through use of a binding process, such as binding arbitration.

Arbitration

Arbitration clauses are common in commercial contracts. Where organizations (or their lawyers) anticipate that the courts may not be an inappropriate forum for resolving disputes, they can include a clause in the agreement referring any dispute to arbitration rather than to the courts.

Arbitration may or may not be more efficient than going to court. In some cases, arbitration can be more expensive and more time-consuming than court, depending on the rules set for the arbitration. However, unless the organizational philosophy favours lengthy hearings, the arbitration clause should provide rules for the arbitration that will limit its time and cost.

Some ideas for reducing time and cost include having only written rather than oral arguments, having no or limited oral discovery, limiting the number of documents that each side can adduce, limiting the number of witnesses, limiting the time for examination and cross-examination, and for opening and closing arguments, and setting the time within which the arbitrator must render a decision. These limitations may come at the cost of some procedural or evidentiary safeguards, but they will result in an efficient resolution of the dispute.

Some organizations will have concerns that agreeing to be bound by strict procedural rules for arbitration, without knowing the issues to be determined in the arbitration, could limit the organization's ability to present its case effectively. This is a valid point; however, if the organization places significant weight on reducing the time and cost associated with arbitration (and dispute resolution in general), it may prefer rules that limit the time for the arbitration, even at the cost of having an incomplete presentation of its own case. Organizations can be reassured by the fact that shortening the arbitration process is just as likely to work in their favour as against them. Furthermore, their lawyers, if required, can usually reduce their case to fit cleanly within prescribed rules.

The clause setting out the rules for the arbitration can also provide that if either organization refuses to participate in the negotiation or mediation, the arbitrator can consider that fact when he or she determines whether either organization should be required to reimburse the other for costs incurred in the dispute resolution process.

Procedure Is Only Procedure To Be Used

The final portion of the ADR clause should state that the organizations agree that the process set out in the clause is the only process to be used, and that they agree that they will not go to court to resolve disputes arising out of the agreement.

The clause could still permit either organization to go to court if necessary to prevent the other from causing irreparable damage.

Length of the ADR Clause

Organizations entering into agreements often prefer short, clear contractual language rather than long convoluted terms. For the ADR clause, that preference must be balanced with the desire to set out specific rules for processes that will be used, so that organizations will not need to argue about the processes once the dispute arises. The clause should be readable and understandable, and yet comprehensive.

An example of a multi-step ADR clause can be found in Appendix A.

INDEPENDENT ORGANIZATIONS THAT CAN ASSIST WITH INTER-ORGANIZATIONAL DISPUTES

In the United States, the Center For Public Resources (CPR) was formed to assist companies to become familiar with ADR and to use ADR options when appropriate. CPR, a non-profit organization, has a CPR Corporate Policy Statement (the Pledge) that provides that the companies that have signed the Pledge agree to attempt to resolve any disputes using ADR processes before resorting to litigation. Many U.S. companies have signed the Pledge. CPR also provides materials about ADR, offers training about ADR, and maintains a panel of mediators, arbitrators, and other neutrals to assist companies to resolve disputes.

In Canada, a similar organization has evolved. The Canadian Foundation for Dispute Resolution (CFDR) has a Protocol similar to the CPR Pledge, a list of independent neutrals, standard rules for arbitrations, and publishes written material about ADR. CFDR also provides its corporate members with a half-day consultation with a systems design specialist about the specific needs of the organization in the field of systems design.

Also, the Arbitration and Mediation Institute of Canada and the American Arbitration Association are large organizations (the former in Canada, the latter in the United States) that can provide disputing organizations with lists of qualified mediators and arbitrators.

S U M M A R Y

ADR IN EXTERNAL DISPUTES

- organizations should plan for external disputes before they arise, by having multi-step ADR clauses in contracts

- the clause should provide for interest-based processes (such as negotiation and mediation), to be followed by rights-based processes (such as mini-trial, early neutral education, and arbitration)

- the final process in the clause should be binding

- if the clause provides for arbitration, it should set out the process for the arbitration in the clause

CHAPTER 14

Concluding
Thoughts

As we move into the 21st century, conflict continues to pervade many aspects of our lives. Organizations are not immune to conflict, and often find themselves faced with significant internal conflict as well as conflict with other organizations.

Conflict in and of itself, is not inherently bad. If it is dealt with productively, effectively, and efficiently, it can help the organization to prosper and evolve. When a systems design team is established to analyze and make recommendations about effective ways of dealing with conflict, the organization is not admitting failure; to the contrary, it is proceeding in a logical and productive way to minimize the cost and time spent dealing with conflict, and maximize the benefits of dealing with it effectively.

ADR systems design is still in its infancy, although it is a rapidly growing field. Systems design teams should not expect to produce ideal ADR systems that can smoothly move an organization from disarray to an organized structure. The design team can, however, use the DIRECT approach to ADR systems design to establish processes that can achieve both short- and long-term benefits for the organization. The processes will inevitably need to be evaluated and improved over time.

For those of us who enjoy being creative and innovative, working towards noble goals such as assisting others to deal with conflict more effectively, and working in exciting and fast-changing fields, ADR systems design can be rewarding and fulfilling.

Sample Multi-Step ADR Clause

RESOLUTION PROCESS

(a) Negotiations

Company A and Company B will attempt to resolve any controversy relating to this Agreement by negotiations between representatives of the parties who have authority to settle the controversy.

The disputing party will give the other party written notice of the dispute. Within five business days of receiving this notice, the receiving party will submit to the other a written response. Neither the notice nor the response shall exceed three pages. The representatives shall meet at a mutually acceptable time and place within five business days of the date of the responding party's notice.

(b) Mediation

If the matter has not been resolved within five business days of the responding party's notice, or if either party will not meet, the dispute will be submitted to mediation as set out below. The mediator will have no power to bind the parties. The mediation will be confidential and without prejudice.

(i) Selection of Mediator

Company A and Company B will have three business days from the end of the time for negotiation to agree upon a mutually acceptable mediator (the "Mediator"). If no Mediator has been selected within that time, Company A and Company B agree jointly to request that [a particular ADR Service Provider in the region] supply within two business days, a list of five potential Mediators. Within two business days of the receipt of the list, Company A and Company B will independently rank the proposed candidates, will simultaneously exchange rankings, and will agree to select as the Mediator the individual receiving the highest combined ranking who is available. If either party does not rank and provide a copy of the ranking to the other party, the party who does rank will be able to select the Mediator from the list.

(ii) Time and Place for Mediation

In consultation with the Mediator, Company A and Company B will designate a mutually convenient time and place for the mediation (and unless circumstances require otherwise, the date should be not later than five business days after the selection of the Mediator).

(iii) Fees of Mediator

The fees of the Mediator will be shared equally by Company A and Company B.

(iv) Termination of Procedure

Company A and Company B agree to participate in the mediation for at least four hours (unless terminated earlier by the Mediator). After that time, either Company A or Company B may leave the mediation at any time. If the mediation does not yield a settlement, Company A and Company B agree not to take any action (other than good faith attempts to negotiate a settlement to the dispute) prior to the conclusion of a five-day post-mediation period that commences on the day after the conclusion of the mediation.

(c) Arbitration

After the expiry of the five-day period referred to in sub-clause (b)(iv), or if either party will not participate in the mediation, the controversy will be finally settled by arbitration in accordance with the provisions of the [relevant legislation]. The following rules will apply to the arbitration.

(i) There will be a single arbitrator (the "Arbitrator"). Company A and Company B will have five business days from the end of the five-day post-mediation period to agree on the Arbitrator. If they cannot agree, either party may request that [a particular ADR service provider in the region] supply a list of five qualified Arbitrators. Within two business days of the receipt of the list, Company A and Company B will independently rank the proposed Arbitrators, will simultaneously exchange rankings, and will agree to select as the Arbitrator the individual receiving the highest combined ranking who is available. If either party does not rank and provide a copy of the ranking to the other party, the party who does rank will be able to select the Arbitrator.

(ii) Company A and Company B will agree, in consultation with the Arbitrator, on the rules for the arbitration. Absent agreement to the contrary, the following rules, designed to save time and expense for the parties, will apply:

    A) Pleadings will be exchanged within 15 days of the selection of the Arbitrator. The disputing party will provide to the other party and the arbitrator within 10 days a statement of their position on the issues. The other party will respond within five days thereafter. Neither document will be more than five pages in length;

B) Each party will provide to the other access to any documents that may be relevant to the arbitration. Each party will also provide to the other, 10 days before the arbitration hearing, a list and copies of up to (but not exceeding) the 15 documents that the party intends to rely on at the arbitration;

C) There will be no oral discovery;

D) The arbitration will take place within two months of the selection of the Arbitrator;

E) At the arbitration hearing, opening argument will be limited to one half hour per party;

F) Each party may produce up to two witnesses for direct examination. The total time permitted for direct examination (whether one or two witnesses is produced) will be two hours. Total time for cross-examination will also be two hours for each company;

G) All evidence is admissible and its weight will be determined by the Arbitrator;

H) Each party may introduce any of its 15 documents;

I) Closing argument will be limited to one hour for each party;

    J) The Arbitrator will attempt to produce a decision within seven calendar days of the conclusion of the arbitration, and written reasons within one month of the arbitration.

(iii) The arbitration will be conducted in English and will take place in [city].

(iv) The arbitration awards will be given in writing and will be final, not subject to any appeal, and will deal with the question of costs of the arbitration. In the award of costs, the Arbitrator may consider each party's effort to resolve the dispute through negotiation and mediation, and any settlement offer made. If either party refuses to participate in the negotiation or mediation, there will be a presumption that solicitor and client costs will be awarded against the party refusing to participate, regardless of the outcome of the arbitration.

(v) Judgment upon the arbitration award may be entered into any court having jurisdiction, or application may be made to such court for judicial recognition of the award.

(vi) The Arbitrator will not award punitive or special damages.

(d) This Procedure is the Only Procedure for Settling Disputes

The procedures specified in this section are the only procedures for the resolution of controversies arising out of or related to this Agreement, or the breach, termination or validity of it, or any other related agreement between Company A and Company B. If either party attempts to have issues resolved in court that should properly be resolved pursuant to this section, the parties agree that this section can be used to stay any such proceedings. However, before or during the time that Company A and Company B follow these procedures, either one can apply to the appropriate court to get an injunction if the party reasonably believes that such a step is necessary to avoid irreparable damage or harm. Even if either party takes such action, both parties will continue to participate in good faith in the procedures set out in this section.

Procedure Manual for Mediation of Credit Disputes Between Bank of Montreal and Small- and Medium-Sized Enterprises (SME's)

[The Manual has been condensed and edited for this appendix.]

Background

1. For the purposes of this program, a Small- or Medium-Sized Enterprise("SME") is defined as an existing commercial borrowing customer of the Bank of Montreal whose outstanding principal indebtedness to the Bank totals $1 million or less. In the discussion below of the Bank's mediation programme, all references to "the Community Banking Manager" or "the CBM" mean the Community Banking Manager or that person's designate.

2. If an SME is dissatisfied with

   (a) the Bank's decision to amend or end an existing financing arrangement,

or (b) the Bank's decision to enforce existing security,

then the SME has the right to appeal to its CBM.

3. If the CBM does not amend the original decision to the SME's satisfaction, then the SME has the right to immediately initiate the Bank's mediation process, outlined herein. The CBM provides the SME with a FirstBank Mediation Request Form to start the process.

   If the mediation does not yield an agreement, then the SME still has the right to appeal to the Office of the Vice-Chairman, or ultimately to the Office of the Superintendent of Financial Institutions.

4. To provide a timely resolution for the SME, deadlines have been set for the various steps within the Bank's mediation process, as summarized in Table 1 (at the end of this document). However, if both the SME and the CBM agree, the time allowed for any step in the process can be extended.

The SME Initiates the Mediation Process

5. The SME must fill out a FirstBank Mediation Request form. This form requests that the Bank try to resolve the credit dispute through mediation.

6. Within two business days after receiving the form, the CBM should give the SME a list of three potential mediators (and their resumes) from the Bank's pre-approved list.

7. (a). The SME will then have three business days to either:

   (i) choose a potential mediator from the CBM's list [see (b) below], or from a further list of pre-approved mediators obtained on request from the CBM; or

   (ii) nominate a mediator not on the list [see (b) below].

   (b) If the SME selects a potential mediator from the CBM's list, the CBM should give the proposed mediator a list of the feasible dates for mediation, being the dates on which the SME and the Bank would both be available for mediation.

   Upon the proposed mediator confirming availability, the CBM will promptly retain the proposed mediator on behalf of the Bank and SME. If the proposed mediator is unavailable, then the CBM should ask the SME to nominate another mediator.

   Until the mediator is retained, no one should inform the proposed mediator of any of the facts in dispute or the issues to be discussed.

   (c) If the SME nominates a potential mediator not on the CBM's list of three names provided to the SME, then the CBM should check whether that person is already on the Bank's larger pre-approved list. If the proposed mediator is on the latter list, then the parties should proceed as outlined in (b) above.

If the proposed mediator is not on the Bank's pre-approved list, then the CBM should see that the proposed mediator meets the criteria of either having mediation training or having experience as a mediator. If the proposed mediator meets the qualification criteria, then the parties should proceed as outlined in (b) above. If the CBM is uncertain as to whether or not the proposed mediator is qualified, the CBM should deem the proposed mediator to be qualified. However, if the proposed mediator clearly does not meet the qualification criteria, then the CBM should ask the SME to nominate another mediator.

Preliminary Matters

8. Normally, the mediation should be within three business days after the mediator is retained; if that is not possible, the mediation must be held no later than 10 business days after the mediator is retained.

9. The mediation may take place at the mediator's offices, or may be held at another place convenient for the parties. The location must be available for at least six hours and must include:

(i) one room sufficiently large for the mediator, the representatives of the SME and the Bank, and any other persons who will attend, to meet together;

(ii) a second room suitable for private discussions; and

(iii) convenient, private access to a telephone.

If suitable meeting facilities are not available, or if it is impractical because of distance for the parties to meet together face-to-face with the mediator, then the mediation may be conducted by telephone. The mediator will determine the appropriate mix of conference calls and private calls when conducting the mediation.

10. The Bank and the SME must give to the mediator and to each other, a summary of the facts and issues surrounding the dispute. The summary should also state who will represent that party at the mediation and who (if anyone) will be attending to provide advice or support to that party. Each summary must be no longer than three pages. A summary should not try to "argue" a party's case, but rather set out the party's concerns and its understanding of the relevant facts. A summary must arrive in each recipients hands at least 24 hours before the mediation.

11. The parties will sign Terms of the Mediation Process setting out the parameters of the mediation.

12. From the time that the SME files the mediation-request form, until the mediation ends,

   (a) the Bank will not take any action to enforce its security (except in extraordinary circumstances as set out below); and

   (b) the SME will not dispose of any of its assets, except in the ordinary course of business, or with the Bank's written permission.

   If the CBM reasonably believes that the SME is disposing of significant assets in violation of (b) above, or that the SME has committed, is committing, or is likely to commit fraud, the CBM may apply to the Divisional Senior Vice-President of the Bank for authorization to abandon the mediation and to immediately enforce the Bank's security.

Persons Attending the Mediation

13. The SME must be represented at the mediation by a person with authority to bind the SME. The CBM may waive this requirement if extraordinary circumstances preclude timely attendance by an SME representative with authority.

14. The SME's account manager and the CBM (or designate) are to attend the mediation. The Bank's representative(s) at the mediation must

   (a) explain the limits of his/her authority to the mediator and to the SME at the start of the mediation [but see para. 15 below]; and

   (b) assure the SME that the SME will not be asked to sign any deal until the proposed resolution has been presented and received concurrence through the head office.

15. Prior to the mediation, the CBM should discuss the matter with the Bank's credit department. Ideally, a person in the Bank's credit department should be available for consultations by telephone during the mediation.

16. Either party may bring legal counsel to the mediation, and/or any other person whom either party would like to have attend for advice or assistance (such as an accountant). Persons who are attending the mediation to advise or assist either party must:

    (i) be invited by the SME or the Bank, with advance notification of attendance to the mediator and the other party;

    (ii) enter into a confidentiality agreement regarding the mediation.

17. All persons whose agreement may be essential to resolving the dispute—such as guarantors—should be strongly encouraged to attend the mediation.

18. Any person attending the mediation should bring whatever materials are considered necessary to resolve the issues being mediated.

The Mediation Process

19. The mediation will be an "interest-based mediation." This means that the mediator will focus on helping the parties to identify their underlying interests and concerns as a basis for negotiating a mutually agreeable resolution. The mediator will not focus exclusively on analyzing the legal rights or legal positions of the parties.

20. The mediator will have no authority to impose any outcome on the parties.

21. The mediation normally will be scheduled to last for six hours, but may run longer or shorter as required.

22. The SME may withdraw from the mediation at any time.

23. At least one representative of the Bank must stay at the mediation for at least four hours, after which the representative is free to leave. It should only be in extremely rare circumstances that all of the Bank's representatives leave before the mediator indicates that the mediation session has ended. During the mediation, the Bank's representatives must use their best efforts to

   (a) listen to the SME's concerns;

   (b) repeat the concerns back to the SME to ensure that the Bank has understood them; and

   (c) attempt to accommodate the SME, subject to satisfying the interests of the Bank.

Expenses

24. A mediator will be paid $200 per hour, to a maximum of $1500 per day. The mediator may additionally charge up to two hours of preparation.

25. The Bank will pay for the first three hours of the mediation proper, and the balance of the fee (including the mediator's preparation time) will be paid equally by the Bank and the SME.

26. If it is necessary to rent facilities for the mediation—such as space at a hotel—then the cost of the facilities will be shared equally by the Bank and the SME. If long-distance telephone charges are entailed during the mediation, those costs will be shared equally by the Bank and the SME.

Mediator Protected

27. Neither party may seek access to the mediator's notes for any purpose.

28. The mediator will not be compellable as a witness in any court proceedings.

Post-Mediation

29. The mediation will be confidential and "without prejudice." No information obtained in the mediation may be used in any subsequent proceeding. Nothing that occurs or is communicated in the mediation may be disclosed outside the mediation, except with the consent of the SME.

30. Outside the mediation, the mediator will not make any recommendation about a possible resolution, except with the consent of the parties concerned.

31. If the mediation yields a resolution to the dispute, the CBM should:

    (i) Assist the mediator to reduce the agreement to writing;

    (ii) If approved by a person or persons having authority to bind the Bank, sign the agreement. Prior review by the Bank's solicitor may be appropriate.

and then

    (iii) Arrange for the SME to sign. If the SME did not have legal counsel at the mediation, then the CBM should suggest that the SME obtain independent legal advice.

The drafting and signing of the agreement should be completed within three days after the mediation.

32. If the mediation does not yield a binding agreement, each party retains all legal rights it had before the mediation. Even if a comprehensive agreement is not reached, the mediator may be able to identify some points of agreement, which should be recorded.

TABLE 1
SCHEDULE OF TEMPORAL MILESTONES
FOR FIRSTBANK MEDIATION PROCESS

Step No.	Description	Days From Prior Step	Total Days From Mediation Request
1.	Bank amends, reduces or cancels SME's existing financing arrangement.		
2.	SME appeals to Community Bank Manager.		
3.	SME files a FirstBank Mediation Request Form.		
4.	CBM gives SME a list of three mediators.	2 days	2 days
5.	SME selects mediator.	3 days	5 days
6.	Parties deliver summaries to mediator and each other (at least 24 hours prior to the mediation).		
7.	Mediation.	10 days	15 days
8.	If the mediation is successful: Draft agreement and obtain signatures of persons with authority to settle.	3 days	18 days

Ontario Human Rights Commission Mediation Procedures Manual

[The Manual has been condensed and edited for this appendix.]

Commission's Mediation System

- The Commission's mediation system is one that draws from the principles of both interest-based and rights-based mediation and is premised on the requirement that each case will be assessed individually to determine the most appropriate mediation approach to be taken in the matter.

- The Commission's mediation process is voluntary.

- Mediation is offered to the parties in the earlier stages of the complaint process—after the complaint has been filed, registered, and served and following receipt of the respondent's response to the complaint.

- Mediation is strictly confidential.

- The Commission encourages prompt resolution of complaints through mediation; it may be in the best interests of all parties to seek an early resolution through mediation.

Public Interest Mandate

- The Commission is obligated by the Ontario Human Rights Code to protect the public interest in a complaint. While the Commission's Human Rights Mediation Officer will remain neutral throughout the mediation process, any agreement reached between the parties must be approved by the Commission to ensure that the interests of the public have been protected. To assist the parties to negotiate an agreement which addresses public interest concerns, the Mediation Officer will be able to provide information regarding whether the public interest in a complaint has been addressed to the likely satisfaction of the Commission.

- If a public interest remedy is required on the face of the complaint and the respondent's initial response to the complaint, the Commission, through its approval process of settlements, will be able to ensure the public interest has been served. If, however, a public interest issue requiring remedy arises in the course of a mediation meeting, and was not evident on the face of the complaint, the Commission will not be able to ensure that the public interest issues have been dealt with given the confidential nature of the mediation process.

- If the parties are ignoring the public interest component, the Mediation Officer will bring this to their attention. Also, if the proposed terms of settlement do not address an identified public interest issue, the Mediation Officer will provide information based on case law and precedents to the parties, regarding the sorts of remedies that the Commission would be looking for to address the matter.

Preparation for Mediation

- Parties will be provided with an information package including material on the following:
  - the complaint process
  - the mediation process—what it is and what happens when resolution is not obtained
  - the confidentiality of the mediation process
  - the voluntary nature of mediation
  - the role of the Commission and the Commission's Mediator
  - the manner in which the Commission will deal with its public interest mandate
- When both parties are agreeable to participate in mediation, they will be required to sign a mediation agreement which includes an agreement that the person attending the mediation has authorization to make binding decisions on settlements.

- The Human Rights Mediation Officer will not have any contact with the parties before mediation. Scheduling of mediation meetings will be the responsibility of another staff member. In addition, should parties have general questions or require general information about mediation and the process in preparation for mediation, a staff member other than the Mediation Officer will provide the information requested.

Records of Mediation

- Information or documentation from the mediation process is confidential and will not form part of the file when transferred to a Human Rights Investigation Officer, nor can it be referenced in any future document that will influence decision making. In addition, the Mediation Officer, shall not discuss information revealed during the mediation process unless otherwise agreed upon by the parties.

Publication of Settlements

- The Commission, in serving the public interest, publicizes settlements that may have broad impact on human rights issues relevant to a particular industry or issue. Because of the confidential nature of the mediation process, the Commission will only publicize settlements resulting from mediation with the consent of both parties.

Role of Commission Mediator

- During mediation, the Mediation Officer serves as an impartial/neutral third party who facilitates the resolution of the complaint.

When to Mediate

- The Regional Manager must determine whether mediation is appropriate, based on the positions of both parties. Circumstances favouring a mediation approach include:

  - Both parties are willing to participate in mediation;
  - The relationship between the parties is important to them;
  - Those involved want to retain control over the outcome;
  - Neither side really wants to be involved in investigation or litigation;
  - Speed is important; and
  - Both sides need the opportunity to be heard.

When Mediation is Not Appropriate

- Circumstances which do not favour a mediation approach include:

  - The complainant or the respondent(s) rejects Mediation and wishes to proceed directly to the formal process of investigation;
  - Neither side is willing to consider settlement;
  - One side is seeking punitive action;

Communication Before Mediation Meeting

- The Commission will not encourage parties to exchange settlement positions before the mediation meeting. However, the parties are not prevented from exchanging settlement proposals between themselves and on their own initiative.

- Matters relating to who should be in attendance at the mediation meeting should be dealt with prior to the meeting day. Parties should know in advance all who will be present at the meeting.

- If a decision is made to invite the parties to participate in the mediation process, a letter should be sent to both parties within one week of receiving the respondent's position in writing, inviting the parties to a mediation meeting within two weeks. The letter should include the following information:

  - date, time and location of proposed meeting
  - the benefits of the mediation process
  - the disadvantages of the alternative procedures
  - the mediator's role (neutral, impartial)
  - what is expected of the parties
  - direction to the respondent(s) that a person in attendance at the mediation meeting must be authorized to make binding settlement decisions
  - propose to mediate agreement

Mediation Plan

- The Mediation Officer must complete a mediation plan which is based only on the complaint and respondent's response to the complaint. In the Mediation Plan, the Mediation Officer will determine whether power imbalances exist, how they will be addressed, the nature of the parties' relationship, and what mediation approach/strategy will be taken (i.e., telephone, face to face, shuttle).

The Mediation Meeting

- The mediation meeting should occur within 90 days from the date the complaint was filed.

- Mediation meetings can occur through face-to-face meetings, through telephone calls using available conferencing technology or through shuttle mediation when the mediator goes back and forth between rooms where the parties are located.

- Face-to-face mediation meetings should be held in a neutral environment (i.e., Commission Offices, other government offices or public buildings) offering no advantage to either party. Interruptions such as phones and people walking in should be prevented.

The Mediation Officer will remain neutral throughout the process.

- If the Mediation Officer is asked to provide his/her opinion on the case, it is recommended that he/she only provide information based in law or precedents, and not provide his/her personal opinion. This approach will bring legitimacy to the process and to the information provided.

- Whenever possible, mediation meetings should begin with both parties present where the Mediation Officer reads the Commission's standard opening statement which explains the mediation process and ground rules to the parties. Whether parties remain together throughout the mediation meeting will be determined on a case by case basis by the Mediation Officer, who will consider the viability of having the parties together or separate.

- The Mediation Officer shall read the Commission's opening statement at the beginning of the mediation to:
  - explain the purpose of the mediation
  - address practical considerations such as breaks
  - clarify the mediator's role
  - describe the structure and ground rules of the meeting

- The Mediation Officer should invite each party to make an initial statement, invite discussion between the parties, and facilitate a spirit of consensus building.

Interpreters

- Any person is entitled to have an interpreter (for language or hearing impaired) present, but the interpreter should be acceptable to all parties and remain neutral throughout the meeting.

Representation of Parties

- Parties have the right to have representation (i.e., legal counsel or a personal representative) and may request that their representatives be present during a mediation meeting. Representatives and/or counsel should be advised that the meeting is not a hearing and that statements are not taken under oath. Information obtained through the mediation process is confidential and "off the record."

- The Mediation Officer may encourage parties to speak on their own behalf rather than having counsel and/or a representative speak on behalf of their client.

- It is the Mediation Officer's responsibility to maintain order at the meeting and to keep the discussion focused on the issues that are directly related to the complaint and its resolution. The Mediation Officer may suspend or terminate the meeting if the parties are unwilling to comply with normal standards of decorum and courtesy.

Inadmissibility of Mediation Evidence

- All mediation meetings are without prejudice and all parties must be informed of this fact at the beginning of the mediation meeting. Any statement made by a party or information resulting from a mediation meeting is confidential and cannot be admitted as evidence at any further stage of the process.

Resolution

- Should mediation lead to an agreed upon settlement, the Mediation Officer should prepare Minutes of Settlement and other appropriate documentation (releases, letters of assurance, etc.) for signature at the meeting.

- A resolution is immediately confirmed by letter to the parties once the Minutes of Settlement are signed and the terms of settlement have been approved by the Commission.

Approval of Statements Obtained through Mediation

- Two types of settlements may require approval if mediation results in resolution of the complaint, Section 43 and administrative approval.

Settlements Requiring S. 43 Approval

• Approval pursuant to Section 43 of the Code is required when the terms of the settlement are not fully manifested; rather there are terms of settlement that must be implemented or manifested at a future date.

• Settlements agreed to between the parties at mediation which involve something that will be done in the future, for example, the installation of a ramp or the creation of a sexual harassment policy, must be forwarded to the mission for approval under Section 43 of the Code.

Settlements Requiring Administrative Approval

• An administrative approval is a decision by a Regional Manager to approve terms of settlement agreed to by the parties to a complaint. In order to be administratively approved, the terms of settlement must be fully manifested at the time the agreement is signed and should not contain anything that must be done in the future. These administratively approved settlements are not reviewed by the Commissioners.

Bibliography

ARTICLES ON ADR SYSTEMS DESIGN

Carnevale, David G., "Root Dynamics of Alternative Dispute Resolution: An Illustrative Case in the U.S. Postal Service," *Public Administration Review*, Sept./Oct. 1993, Vol. 53, No. 5. [The Post Office has experimented with an ADR system that incorporates interest-based approaches to disputes that were traditionally resolved by rights-based arbitration. This article discusses the system.]

Cloke, Kenneth, "Conflict Resolution Systems Design, The United Nations, And The New World Order," *8 Mediation Quarterly*, No. 4, Summer, 1991, p. 343. [The author of this article applies the principles from *Getting Disputes Resolved* to the United Nations context and suggests how systems design could be used by the U.N.]

Coates, Mary Lou, Gary T. Furlong, and Bryan M. Downie, *Conflict Management & Dispute Resolution Systems in Canadian Nonunionized Organizations*, Industrial Relations Centre, Queen's University, 1997. [This empirical look at ADR systems in the nonunionized workplace provides observations from 11 Canadian companies about the use of ADR in the workplace.]

Costantino, Cathy A., "Using Interest-Based Techniques to Design Conflict Management Systems," *Negotiation Journal*, Vol. 12, No. 3, July 1996, p. 207. [In this article, Cathy Costantino sets out principles for using interest-based approaches to the design of an ADR system.]

Cronin-Harris, Catherine, "Mainstreaming: Systematizing Corporate Use of ADR" (1995-96), *59 Albany Law Rev.* (No. 3), p. 847. [This academic article traces the history of corporate use of ADR in the United States.]

Goldberg, Stephen B., and Jeanne M. Brett, "Getting, Spending—and Losing—Power in Dispute Systems Design," *Negotiation Journal*, Vol. 7, No. 2, April 1991, p. 119. [Goldberg and Brett discuss a systems design exercise where they were retained to facilitate a conflict between a sales division and a development division of a company.]

Goldberg, Stephen B., and Jeanne M. Brett, "Disputants' Perspectives on the Differences Between Mediation and Arbitration," *Negotiation Journal*, Vol. 6, No. 3, July 1990, p. 249. [This article is the result of a study of the use of mediation and arbitration by the United Mine Workers of America, and discusses some of the benefits of mediation over arbitration.]

Macfarlane, Julie, *Court-Based Mediation of Civil Cases: An Evaluation of the Ontario Court (General Division) ADR Centre*, Queen's Printer for Ontario, 1995. [The Ontario government commissioned Professor Macfarlane to assess the Pilot Project for mandatory mediation in Toronto. This report sets out her findings.]

Manring, Nancy J., "ADR and Administrative Responsiveness: Challenges for Public Administrators," *Public Administration Review*, March/April, 1994, Vol. 54, No. 2. [This article examines how federal legislation in the U.S. relating to ADR for federal agencies has affected the U.S. Forest Service.]

Mazadoorian, Harry N., "On Implementing ADR: One Company's Experience Putting Theory into Practice," *The Complete Lawyer*, Spring, 1987, p. 45. [This article was written by the ADR Manager at CIGNA Corporation (an insurance company) about its ADR system and the successes that he had seen as a result of the system.]

McDermott, E. Patrick, "Using ADR to Settle Employment Disputes," 50 Jan. Disp. Resol. J., p. 8. [This article is a report of a survey of a number of U.S. companies on the extent to which they use ADR processes.]

Negotiation Journal, April 1996, Vol. 12, No. 2. [This volume of the *Negotiation Journal* has a special section that contains numerous articles about ADR in the workplace.]

O'Connor, David, "The Design of Self-Supporting Dispute Resolution Programs," *Negotiation Journal*, Vol. 8, No. 2, April 1992, p. 85. [The article discusses the work of the Massachusetts Office of Dispute Resolution in matching organizations that need help resolving disputes with ADR service providers.]

Rowe, Mary P., "The Ombudsman's Role in a Dispute Resolution System," *Negotiation Journal*, Vol. 10, No. 4, October 1994, p. 353. [This article discusses the ombudsman's role in corporations, and how the ombudsman can assist with problem solving in times of change.]

Sander, Frank E. A., and Stephen B. Goldberg, "Fitting the Forum to the Fuss: A User Friendly Guide to Selecting an ADR Procedure," *Negotiation Journal*, Vol. 10, No. 1, January 1994, p. 49. [As its title indicates, this article provides factors to consider when selecting which ADR process is appropriate. It also discusses common barriers to settlement.]

Singer, Linda, Michael Lewis, Alan Houseman, and Elizabeth Singer, "Alternative Dispute Resolution and the Poor, Part II: Dealing with Problems in Using ADR and Choosing a Process," *Clearinghouse Review*, July, 1992, p. 288. [This article examines the use of ADR by the poor, and addresses the choice of the appropriate ADR process for specific issues. It also looks at the qualifications of ADR neutrals and the appropriate evaluation of an ADR project.]

Slate, William K., and George H. Friedman, "Ten Things Not To Do When Designing An Employment ADR System," *HR Advisor*, January/February 1997, Vol. 2, No. 4. [This brief article presents a list of pitfalls employers can encounter when creating ADR systems.]

"Dispute Resolution and the Securities Industry" (1987), 42 Arbit. J. 15. [This is a bibliography of articles on ADR in the securities industry. Most of the articles relate to arbitration programs.]

Slaikeu, Karl A., and Ralph H. Hasson, "Not Necessarily Mediation: The Use of Convening Clauses in Dispute Systems Design," *Negotiation Journal*, Vol. 8, No. 4, October 1992, p. 331. [This article discusses the idea of putting a "convening clause" in a contract to deal with potential disputes.]

BOOKS

SYSTEMS DESIGN

Costantino, Cathy A., and Christina Sickles Merchant, *Designing Conflict Management Systems*, Jossey-Bass Inc., 1996. [This book on ADR systems design takes the theories developed by Ury, Brett and Goldberg and incorporates ideas from the fields of Organizational Behaviour and Organizational Development.]

Feld, Lisa, and Peter A. Simm, *Complaint-Mediation In Ontario's Self-Governing Professions*, The Fund For Dispute Resolution, 1995. [The College of Physicians and Surgeons of Ontario have a system where mediation is used to help resolve complaints against physicians. This study examines the system.]

Ury, William L., Jeanne M. Brett, and Stephen B. Goldberg, *Getting Disputes Resolved*, Jossey-Bass Inc., 1988. [This is the first and pre-eminent book in the field of ADR systems design. It discusses the differences between interests, rights, and power in the context of designing ADR systems for organizations.]

NEGOTIATION

Fisher, Roger, William L. Ury, and Bruce Patton, *Getting to Yes: Negotiating Agreement Without Giving In*, Second Edition, Penguin, 1992. [The seminal book on negotiation written in the last twenty years presents, develops and discusses the theory of principled negotiation.]

Fisher, Roger, and Scott Brown, *Getting Together: Building Relationships as We Negotiate*, Penguin, 1991. [This book presents the ways that negotiators can deal with their emotions and negotiate in a way that preserves rather than destroys relationships.]

Fisher, Roger, Elizabeth Kopelman, and Andrea Kupfer Schneider, *Beyond Machiavelli*, Harvard University Press, 1994. [This book, subtitled *Tools for Coping with Conflict*, presents and discusses the seven elements of principled negotiation, often focusing on international conflict.]

Fisher, Roger, and Danny Ertel, *Getting Ready to Negotiate*, Penguin, 1995. [This workbook presents a structured approach to preparing for negotiation, using the seven elements.]

Lax, David, and James Sebenius, *The Manager as Negotiator*, Free Press, 1986. [This book focuses on negotiation from the perspective of a manager within an organization.]

Raiffa, Howard, *The Art and Science of Negotiation*, Harvard University Press, 1982. [This book presents a mathematical approach to negotiation, focusing on game theory and economic analysis.]

Ury, William L., *Getting Past No: Negotiating With Difficult People*, Bantam, 1991. [This book presents ideas for people who must negotiate with competitive and difficult negotiators.]

ADR

Ross, Norman A., *You Be The Judge: The Complete Canadian Guide to Resolving Legal Disputes Out of Court*, John Wiley & Sons Canada Ltd., 1997. [This book presents and discusses some of the ADR processes, and how they can be used to resolve legal disputes. There is particular emphasis on mediation.]

Singer, Linda, *Settling Disputes*, Westview Press, 1990 [This book discusses how ADR processes can be used for family, business, consumer, employment, and community disputes.]

Stitt, Allan J. (editor), *Alternative Dispute Resolution Practice Manual*, CCH Canadian Ltd., loose leaf. [This manual is a collection of articles on ADR processes, ADR applications, issues for ADR professionals, and a collection of Canadian legislation, forms and precedents. It is updated four times yearly.]

ADR TRAINING

Patton, Bruce, *On Teaching Negotiation*, Program On Negotiation Working Paper Series, Harvard, 1984. [Bruce Patton's paper that he wrote as a third year student at Harvard Law School discusses the ways to teach principled negotiation. The paper is available through the Program on Negotiation at Harvard Law School.]

MEDIATION

Baruch Bush, Robert A., and Joseph P. Fogler, *The Promise of Mediation*, Jossey-Bass, 1994. [This book on mediation is best known for its presentation of the transformative nature of mediation.]

Domenici, Kathy, *Mediation: Empowerment in Conflict Management*, Waveland Press, Inc., 1996. [This short, easy to read book provides information about the stages of mediation and describes the mediation process.]

Moore, Christopher W., *The Mediation Process*, Second Edition, Josey-Bass, 1996 [This book, written by a leading U.S. scholar in mediation, provides an in-depth analysis of the mediation process and how to act as a mediator in it.]

ARBITRATION

Casey, J. Brian, *International and Domestic Commercial Arbitration*, Carswell, 1993. [This is a comprehensive text on Canadian law of commercial arbitration, updated twice yearly.]

Index